Syriac

Maccabees

Deuterocanonical Books

SCRIPTURAL RESEARCH INSTITUTE
Published by Digital Ink Productions, 2024

Copyright

Syriac Maccabees - Deuterocanonical Books

First edition. September 6, 2024

Copyright © 2024 Scriptural Research Institute

ISBN: 978-1-998288-87-8

Lady Shamoni and the Maccabean Martyrs, also known as 6th Maccabees, and The Story of the Lady and her Seven Sons, also known as 7th Maccabees, are a ancient Syriac texts, which share a source with Septuagint's 2nd Maccabees. 8th Maccabees is a section of the Chronographia by John Malalas, written in Greek in the mid 6th century AD, based on Syriac sources. These English translations were created by the Scriptural Research Institute in 2024.

The image used for the cover is an artistic reinterpretation of 'The Siege and Destruction of Jerusalem by the Romans Under the Command of Titus' by David Roberts, painted in 1850.

Table of Contents

Forward

The Syrian tradition churches of the Middle East and South Asia, have maintained several deuterocanonical books that are not included in the Peshitta, the standard Syriac version of the Christian Bible. While the Peshitta continues to be the standard form of the Christian Bible for many Asian churches, including the Assyrian Church of the East, Chaldean Catholic Church, Malankara Orthodox Syrian Church, Maronite Church, Syriac Catholic Church, Syriac Orthodox Church, Syro-Malabar Church, Syro-Malankara Catholic Church, and Thozhiyoor Church, these various churches have also maintained additional ancient Christian texts some of which have been studied by Western scholars in the past few centuries.

The consensus within Western biblical scholarship is that the Old Testament of the Peshitta was translated into Syriac from the Hebrew Tanakh, probably in the 2nd century AD, and that the New Testament of the Peshitta was translated from Koine Greek, probably in the early 5th century, with the disputed books being added in 616 AD. However, this interpretation of its origin is based on the Byzantine Orthodox Church's viewpoint and is not the traditional viewpoint of the Syrian churches. The traditional Syrian viewpoint is that the Peshitta's Old Testament is a transcription from the older Aramaic versions of the books, which the Hebrew translation is also based on.

While the older books in the Tanakh were likely composed in Canaanite, either by Samaritans or Judahites, the later books, such as Daniel and Esther, would have been composed in Aramaic before being translated into Classical Hebrew alongside the older Canaanite books. The translation of Daniel was never completed, leaving the mixed Hebrew and Aramaic language book found in the Masoretic text. The earliest sanctioned Aramaic translation of the Torah appears to have happened during the rule of King Manasseh of Judah, who first removed the name of God from the texts according to the Talmud's Sanhedrin 103b. This is almost certainly where some of the differences between the later Greek and Hebrew translations originated. The Greek translations made at the Library of Alexandria were based on the common Aramaic versions of the books, while the Hebrew translations appear to be translated from Canaanite texts.

Based on the interpretation found in the Talmud's Megillah 3a, the Aramaic translation of the Torah was used in the temple at the time of Nehemiah, who arrived in Jerusalem in approximately 385 BC. As Aramaic was the common language of the era, this does correlate with the archeological evidence. The papyrus manuscripts found at Oxyrhynchus, in central Egypt include correspondence between the temple in Jerusalem and the temple in Elephantine from circa 419 BC, and were written in Aramaic. Most of the latter books of the Masoretic text and Septuagint were likely composed in Aramaic, including Ezra-Nehemiah, Esther, Maccabees, and parts of Daniel.

The Peshitta includes Syriac translations of the four books of the Maccabees found in the Septuagint, along with a 5th book of Maccabees, which is also labelled as *The History Of The Destruction Of Jerusalem*. This book is a Syriac translation of the 6th book of Josephus' *The Judean War*. General Josephus had started on the Judean side of the rebellion, however, was captured by the Romans, and survived the war. During the fall of Jerusalem, he was part of Caesar Titus' entourage who tried to negotiate with the Judean rebels in Jerusalem. After the destruction of Jerusalem, Josephus was given some of the surviving archives and wrote *Antiquities of the Judeans*, as well as *The Judean War*. These books survive in Greek; however, it is generally agreed that Josephus wrote these books in Judeo-Aramaic, and then translated them into Greek, as the audience he was writing to was the Judean diaspora in the Middle East. The Syrian churches have traditionally claimed that the

Peshitta's 5th Maccabees is a Syriac transliteration of Josephus' original Aramaic text.

The Peshitta's 5th Maccabees is often confused with the Arabic book of Maccabees in English literature due to a misidentification by the Anglican historian Henry Cotton in 1832. Josephus' writing is also part of the Ge'ez language extended canon of the Ethiopian bible, however, the Ge'ez translations are longer, and it is debated if they were made from the old Aramaic versions or an Arabic translation.

5th Maccabees seems to have been added to the Peshitta in order to create a conclusion to the history of the kingdom of Judea, as it is only the section of *The Judean War* which covers the conquest of Jerusalem and the destruction of the Temple. Josephus' intent was to accurately record the fall of Judea and is generally considered a reliable source. Not all of the 1st century historians agreed with Josephus' view of what happened.

Justus of Tiberias was a 1st century Jewish historian who had been the secretary of King Herod Agrippa II, the last ruler of the Herodian dynasty who reigned over territories outside of Judea as a Roman client. Agrippa II fled Jerusalem in 66 AD, during the Judean uprising, and supported the Roman side in the First Judean-Roman War. His work has not survived to the present, however, Josephus mentioned in his autobiography that he was rebutting some of the claims of Justus in his *History of the Judean War*, meaning Justus' view of Josephus was not favorable. As Josephus had been a Judean general early in the war, Justus' view of him as one of the causes of the war would have been justified. According to Josephus' biography, he surrendered to the Romans after being trapped in a cave with his Judean soldiers, who didn't want to surrender to the Romans. He ordered a mass suicide, and then left the cave and surrendered to the Romans when his soldiers were dead. As this was Josephus' account, which he defended, Justus' account must have been far more scathing.

Although Justus had not been mentioned in Josephus' earlier work, *The Judean War*, Josephus wrote over 30 pages in his autobiography attacking Justus. He accused him of being one of the chief causes of the war, leading attacks on Greeks in Galilee before the war began, but then becoming noncommittal after the war had started, and ultimately serving Agrippa on the Roman side. One of Josephus' claims was that Justus' *History of the Judean War* was filled with errors, but does not discuss them in detail. Josephus claimed that Justus' work lacked facts because Justus did not have access to the field notes of Vespasian and Titus, which suggests that Justus' work was written from the Judean perspective, and ignored the Roman perspective, unlike Josephus' work. Justus also wrote the *Chronicle of the Judean Kings*, which survived until the 9th century, but its content is unknown today.

Josephus' view was certainly pro-Roman by the end of the war, claiming that Emperor Titus went to great lengths to preserve both the city and temple, which was ultimately burned by the Jewish factions. The rebellion in Judea was started by rival factions, led by Simon and John, who Josephus referred to as tyrants. Josephus' account also reports that the burning of both the city and the outer courtyards of the temple was initiated by these tyrants, not the Romans. Ultimately, Titus chose to destroy the city and sold the majority of the survivors as slaves, or sentenced them to be worked to death in the mines of Egypt.

Josephus reported that this was the second time the temple was destroyed, the first time was when the Babylonians conquered the city, and that it was the fifth time the city had been conquered since King David captured it. While this matches the historical texts in the Tanakh and Septuagint, Josephus made one major deviation from the Tanakh, when he claimed the first temple was built by King Melchizedek instead of King Solomon. He dated the building of the first temple to 2106 BC, although the source of his date is not clear. Earlier in the text, he claimed that Solomon laid the foundations of the First Temple in approximately 1059 BC, which is around a century earlier than generally accepted.

Melchizedek was the name of the king of Salem in the Torah, which an ancient scribal note identified as the old name of Jerusalem. If Salem was the ancient name of Jerusalem, it must have preceded the Egyptian Middle Kingdom era, as the city was already known as Ůrůšalim (𓂋𓊪𓈙𓃭𓐍), an Egyptian transliteration of the Old Akkadian name Úru Šalim^{ki} (𒌷𒊩𒅆𒆠), meaning 'light setting land.'

Josephus' minimizing Solomon, a king known from the Tanakh as an idolator, while giving credit to Melchizedek, a king known from the Torah as being honorable, suggests he was a follower of the Sadducee philosophy. Josephus mentioned there being two high priests in Jerusalem during the rebellion: Joseph and Jesus, however, he did not specify which sects they belonged to. Both sects were essentially irradicated during the war, however, the general beliefs of the Pharisees continued into rabbinical Judaism. The older Sadducee sect primarily used the Aramaic language and the Torah, but not the other ancient books commonly known as the Tanakh. The Sadducees sect was also named after the word ṣdq (צדק), meaning 'righteous-ness,' which was also the name of the god that

Melchizedek was named after ṣdq (ץﬧﭏ). The later Pharisee sect developed after Judea gained its independence,
and used both the Torah and the Tanakh as their scriptures. These texts formed the basis of the Rabinnical sect
of Judaism after the destruction of Jerusalem. The Pharisees also used the Hebrew translations of the texts,
although most predominantly spoke Aramaic.

By the time of the rebellion, there were three major
political factions, the Hellenistic Judeans, which included
Josephus, the Zealots, led by Eleazar bar Simon, and the
Sicarii, led by Menahem bar Judah. The Zealots had been
viewed as an extremist group for decades, as they were
xenophobic, and wanted to drive the non-Judahites out
of Judea. The Sicarii were a violent offshoot of the
Zealots, who believed in killing all non-Judeans. Sicarii is
the plural of sicarius, which translates as 'assassin.' The
Latin word was imported into Judeo-Aramaic as the
name Syqryym (סיקריים), and therefore continues to be
used as the historical name of the political faction. The
Hellenistic Judeans largely descended from the Sadducee
philosophy of Judaism, which taught that the Judeans
could live alongside the non-Judeans, as long as they
continued to follow their laws found in the Torah.
Unfortunately, the war was so devastating to the Judean
population that the Sadducee philosophy was essentially

irradicated, leaving Pharisee and Zealot viewpoints to dominate the development of Rabbinical Judaism.

Josephus' writings survive to the present due to Christian scholars preserving them, as he was viewed as a traitor in the later Rabbinical tradition for not committing suicide with his troops. It was forbidden to translate his work into Hebrew, and therefore, there is no medieval Jewish version of his writings, unlike *Josippon* (ספר יוסיפון) and *Jashur* (ספר הישר), both of which are also generally accepted as being composed in Southern Italy, *Josippon* in the 10th century, and *Jashur* in the 16th century. The anonymous author of the *Josippon* claimed to be copying the ancient writings of Joseph ben Gorion (יוסף בן גוריון), which is generally assumed to be a reference to Josephus, however, Josephus' father's name was Matthias. The association of these two men named Joseph/Josephus first appeared in the scribal notes in a copy of the Latin language version of *On the Destruction of Jerusalem*. The 4th century book itself identifies a prefect in Jerusalem as Josephum Gorione Genitum, which the scribe claimed in the notes was Josephus. While the connection with Josephus is generally ignored by historians, *On the Destruction of Jerusalem* does support the existence of Joseph ben Gorion in Jerusalem during the same era as Josephus. The Josippon is a chronicle of Jewish history from Adam to the 1st century AD, ending during the reign of Emperor Titus who ruled Rome between 79 and 81 AD. This suggests it was originally written during his rule.

Fortunately, Josephus' writings survive in Greek, Syriac, Latin, Arabic, and Ge'ez, unlike most of the authors from his era. He describes the destruction of Jerusalem in vivid detail and places the blame on the Zealots and Sicarii, not the Romans. This would have made his books unpopular among the early Rabbinical Jews and is likely why they were banned from being translated into Hebrew.

In addition to the five books of the Maccabees found within the Peshitta, there is additional Syriac literature associated with the woman and her seven sons, who were tortured to death by King Antiochus. In this literature, she is named Shamoni, and her sons are known as the Maccabean martyrs. This concept appears to have developed in the Syriac tradition before the full text of the four Maccabees books in the Septuagint were translated into Syriac in the 5th century AD. The particular Maccabees books in the Septuagint were written in Greek, although they drew on older Aramaic and Judahite literature that is now lost. In the Greek, Hebrew, and Arabic books about the Maccabees, the seven martyrs are never referred to as the Maccabees, this term is used to refer to the followers of Judas, several decades later.

The most famous of these Syriac works is the poem *Lady Shamoni and the Maccabean Martyrs*, which Western biblical scholars have dubbed 6th Maccabees. The poem goes into more detail regarding the torture of the sons of Shamoni than 2nd Maccabees, where the author skipped over most of the gruesome details and then ended the chapter with "This is enough about the eating of sacrifices and the extreme tortures." A lesser-known Syriac work is *The Story of the Lady and her Seven Sons*, which Western biblical scholars have dubbed 7th Maccabees. 7th Maccabees is probably the older of the two, as it does not refer to the seven martyrs as the Maccabees, which is common in Syriac Christian literature. This isn't clear, as the reference to the seven martyrs as 'the Maccabean Martyrs' is found in the title of 6th Maccabees, and not the text itself. The title is likely something created by the Christian editor.

The medieval era *Book of the Hammer*, also called Hebrew Maccabees, repeats the torture found in 2nd Maccabees without the additional details from 6th and 7th Maccabees, indicating that either the texts were unknown to the Hebrew translator, or, they were rejected by him. Hebrew Maccabees uses terminology that indicates that the Hebrew text was prepared from a combination of Greek and Canaanite texts in Visigoth-occupied Spain, sometime between 418 and 439 AD. The Hebrew text was certainly prepared by a Jew, as Christians were not using Hebrew, and later preserved by Jews until it was bought by the Bodleian Library at Oxford, in 1887. The author may have rejected 6th and 7th Maccabees as they were being used by Christians, but it is more likely he did not know of the texts' existence, as they do not appear to have ever been widely distributed outside of the Syriac churches.

Hebrew Maccabees was used as a source for Arabic Maccabees around 525 AD, which also doesn't use any of the additional details found in 6th or 7th Maccabees. While the author of Arabic Maccabees used several sources to compile her history of the Hasmonean dynasty, including Greek, Hebrew, and Latin texts, she does not appear to have known of the existence of 6th or 7th Maccabees. Her 'history' is the least historically accurate of the various books of Maccabees, even though she had access to more accurate texts. Her 'history' appears to have been written in Palestinian Aramaic for Jewish children, as a somewhat fantastical tale of the Hasmonean dynasty, and was later translated into Arabic by a Christian in the early Islamic era. She liberally drew details from many sources, including the tale of King Hannibal from Hebrew Maccabees, which she expanded upon by drawing details from a Latin book on General Hannibal. If she had access to 6th and 7th Maccabees, she certainly would have included some element of the extended torture or dialogue, however, there are no indicators that she knew of their existence.

The text of 6th Maccabees is itself somewhat confusing. Scholars agree the original text was the third-person perspective historical narrative that forms most of the text, however, this is repeatedly interrupted by an editor who interjects their own thoughts in first-person perspective. The editor was clearly a Christian, as he references Jesus, however, even the Christian edits use a mix of terms that confuse their dating. It is entirely plausible that more than one Christian editor handled the poem.

The earliest edits might have been by a Syrian God-Fearer or an Essene Jew before the time of Jesus, or a very early Christian before the destruction of the second temple, as the temple is referred to as the 'altar on the Jebusite section.' This is consistent with the early Jerusalem-Christian rejection of the Levitical priesthood, and the claims to be descended from the priesthood of Melchizedek, the old Jebusite priesthood in Jerusalem, as the Jebusites occupied Jerusalem before the Judahites occupied the city. This does not necessarily mean that the first editor was a Christian, as Josephus also referred to the original temple in Jerusalem as having been built by Melchizedek instead of Solomon, and Josephus was regarded as being a Jew. Based on his writings, Josephus was probably a Saduccee, although he does not self-identify as one. Based on the writing of Josephus, Philo of Alexandria, and Pliny the Elder, the third major sect of Jews at the time was the Essenes (Ἐσσηνοί), who believed they were descendents of ancient Canaanites and had lived in Judea for a thousand generations. Therefore, the reference in the text to the temple as the 'altar on the Jebusite section,' could have been a Jew, early-Christian, or Syrian God-Fearer.

The God-Fearers were a sect that originated in Syria and spread to the Greeks and Romans. They worshiped the sky god, known as Shamayin (𐤔𐤌𐤉𐤍), Uranus (Οὐρανός), and Caelus, who they believed was also the Israelite god. This was probably a continuation of the Neo-Sumerian cult of the sky [deity]An (✳✳), whose name was pronounced as Šamû in Assyrian and Babylonian. They were recorded as early converts to the Pauline sect of Christianity, which originated in Syria and spread to Anatolia and then Greece and Italy. There is evidence that they were active in Syria for centuries before the time of Paul, as there are references to them in the Psalms of David as those 'who fear the skies' (שָׁמַיִם).

However, an editor later uses the term anti-Christ to refer to King Antiochus, which would date the later edits to the era after the emergence of the concept of the anti-Christ in the 2nd century AD. It is unlikely that this phrase originated in the Judean concept of the false Messiah, as no one would have called Antiochus a Messiah, and so he could not be identified as a false Messiah. An editor also referenced Josephus as not including the details about the torture of all of the youths, indicating that this editor lived after the second temple was destroyed, however, this is inconsistence with the earlier reference to the 'altar on the Jebusite section,' supporting a minimum of two redactors, both writing in the first-person. In this translation, the first-person edits are italicized, however, it is not clear how many editors there were.

The older third-person historical narrative appears to be pre-Christian, as it is consistent with Judean writings from the Second Temple era. The focus of the story returns consistently to the preservation of the Orit, the Aramaic version of the Torah that was in use before the Hasmonean dynasty translated and standardized the ancient Samaritan, Judahite, and Aramaic texts into Classical Hebrew. Some scholars believe that this older historical narrative is drawn from the same source the author of 2nd Maccabees used, which is why it retains more of the details. This is conjectural, as the details may be fictional additions to the story found in 2nd Maccabees. However, the author of 2nd Maccabees claimed to be condensing Jason of Cyrene's five-volume work on the Maccabees and certainly skipped over some of the torture. Jason of Cyrene's work is lost, and so this may be a section of his work that was later converted into a Syriac Christian poem.

The historical narrative was certainly translated or transcribed into Syriac at some point, either from Greek or from the older Aramaic script. The third-person narrative and first-person edits use conflicting terminology, where the editor uses terms drawn from Hebrew, like Sheol (ܫܝܘܠ), whereas the older narrative uses terms drawn from Greek, like Tartarus (ܛܪܛܪܘܣ). Tartarus (Τάρταρος) was the ancient Greek translation for Sheol (שְׁאוֹל), the name of the underworld in Judean mythology. While the presence of the word Tartarus in the text could be interpreted as signs of an older Greek manuscript being used as the source, the word Tartarus had been adopted into Aramaic before the era of the story, and, therefore, could have been in either Jason's original work on the Maccabees, or have been used by the original Syriac transcriber as a translation for Sheol.

The Christian editor appears to not know the difference between Sheol / Tartarus and Hades / Gehenna, as the two places are confused in the Christian additions. Sheol and Tartarus were described as dark forgotten realms in Classical literature, as far beneath the world as the land is from the sky. Conversely, the realms of Hades and Gehenna were firey abodes, where the Hinn resided. This indicates that the later Syriac editor was not living at the same time as the early editor, as this mistake is unlikely to have been made until the late-Classical era, after the rise of Christianity in the Roman empire.

The editors provide a long preface to the older narrative that switches between first and third-person perspectives and refers to the origin of the story being Paul, presumably the Christian disciple Paul, although that is not clarified. They also include the names of the youths who were killed as well as their mother, however, they also seem to believe that these youths were Judas and his brothers, who led the revolt against Greek rule in Judea. Two of the youths are named 'Maccabee,' and 'Gaddi,' which were the nicknames of Judas and his brother John. The family is also identified as being the sons of the high priest Matthias, like Judas and his brothers. Clearly, Judas and his brothers did not get tortured to death before starting their rebellion, and so editors must have not understood the history of the Maccabean Revolt.

The errors in this work, in comparison to all other sources, including Christian, Jewish, and non-religious, have generally left it abandoned by scholars. It may have been introduced to the God-Fearer community by Paul of Tarsus, or that could simply be a reference to the idea that he had taken a copy of a book about the Maccabees with him to Damascus. It could be a relic of Jason of Cyrene's work on the Maccabees, or simply fiction. All other known sources besides 7th Maccabees drew from 2nd Maccabees, whose author admittedly skipped over part of the torture in his attempt to abridge the work of Jason, which means this could be a fragment of Jason's work, but if so it has been reworked by those who did not understand the context. As a result, while most modern scholars are willing to accept the oldest sections of text might have started with Jason or another contemporary writer, the poem contains no historical value, as it is unclear how much was edited.

The poem only survives in Syriac, and does not appear to have been translated into other languages before the 1800s. The older Jewish sections are theorized to have originated in an early Jewish piyyut (פִּיּוּט), which is a poem that is sung, chanted, or recited during religious services. The era in which the piyyut originated is unclear, as is the era of the Christian additions. Different scholars have estimated the dating of the Christian poem to as early as the 1st century AD, or as late as the 19th century, right before the text was discovered by Western academics. Several copies were documented in the 1800s, however, only one is still publically available, and it is the source of all translations. This manuscript is at the Bodleian Library at Oxford and is designated as Or. 624 (Syr. 134). It was purchased from the Christian community of Malabar in India and is written in the East Syriac Madnhāyā script which is still used by the Syriac Christian churches in India. Madnhāyā (ܡܲܕܢܚܵܝܵܐ) was the form of the Syriac script that developed from the Classical era Estrangēlā script during the Sasanian Empire, between 224 and 637 AD. This may indicate the origin of the Christian additions, as the dodecasyllabic meter is similar to the work of Jacob of Serugh who died in 521 AD.

The older Jewish piyyut could have been composed at any point between the era of the events and the Christian reworking, however, did almost certainly originate in a form of Aramaic, such as Judeo-Aramaic or Syriac. The surviving Madnhāyā manuscript does not clarify which dialect the older piyyut was in, however, it does include the name Tartarus, suggesting it was composed in Syriac, and not Judeo-Aramaic. There is a curiosity in the piyyut section of the poem, which points to a very early composition in the 1st or 2nd century AD, in that it refers to the death of the three youths in Daniel as having happened in Assyria. In the Septuagint's and Masoretic versions of the book of Daniel, the three youths were killed in Babylon. However, the 1st century addition to the Septuagint known as 4th Maccabees also claimed they were killed in Assyria. 4th Maccabees was probably composed in Greek, however, was written by a Jew, likely a Pharisee. This indicates that during the 1st century, it was accepted by some Jews that the events happened in Assyria and not Babylon.

This linguistic anomaly found in texts dating to the 1st and 2nd centuries was most likely caused by the influence of the Greek language. The Greeks did use the name Assyria (Ἀσσυρία) for the lands of ancient Assyria, however, the ancient lands of Babylon were called Mesopotamia (Μεσοποταμία). The ancient city of Babylon had been supplanted by the Greek capital of Ctesiphon, and the concept of Babylonia had become archaic, replaced by the concept of Mesopotamia. When the Roman Emperor Trajan occupied the region during his campaigns against the Parthians, between 115 and 116 AD, he divided the region into the provinces of Armenia, Assyria, and Mesopotamia, based on the common Greek names used in the region.

This does not prove the piyyut dates to the era, however, it is an indicator. If so, the piyyut makes sense as a remembrance of the martyrs from the Greek occupation of Judea, as the Judeans were struggling with the Romans at the time. The Judean-Roman wars spanned 66 to 136 AD. In the First Judean-Roman War, Jerusalem was sacked and the Second Temple was destroyed.

The second war was the Kitos War, which started while Trajan was fighting the Parthians in Mesopotamia. The Jews in Mesopotamia had fought for the Parthian Empire and refused to switch to the Roman side after the Parthians were defeated, leading to a massive slaughter of Mesopotamian Jews by the Roman general Lusius Quietus. This resulted in Jewish rebels attacking the Roman legions in Egypt, Cyprus, and Cyrene, and massacred the Romans living in those provinces. The general population did not rebel, and so the Romans were able to reoccupy the provinces. The rebels fled to Judea and amassed at the town of Lod, where they were ultimately defeated and executed. The third war was the Bar Kokhba revolt, also called the Second Judean-Roman War, as the war was in Judea again. This war spanned 132 to 136 AD. It resulted in a Roman victory and a virtual extermination of the Judean population. Most of the Judean survivors were sold as slaves to other countries, and the idea of Judea was permanently removed from Roman maps, replaced with the province of Palestine.

It took centuries for the Jewish population to recover in Palestine, however, they were populous enough to form a rebellion against Constantinople during the Civil War of 350-353. It wasn't much of a rebellion, capturing only a small region of Galilee, however, the Jews of that region were mass slaughtered by the Byzantine army after being defeated. While it's possible the piyyut was composed this late, it seems less likely. Greek had been supplanted by Middle Persian in Mesopotamia at this point, and the region was known as Ôyrq (ܚܝܕܩ) in Syriac, based on the Persian name Åᵢrg (ܢܕܝܓ). Additionally, the Judeans were again in conflict with the Greeks. While the remembrance of the earlier martyrs during Greek rule seems consistent, using a borrowed Greek work like Tartarus is inconsistent. All of this points to an origin during the Judean-Roman Wars.

Conversely, 7th Maccabees does not appear to have been significantly altered by Christians. There is a reference to the youths believing in the Messiah that is often assumed to be a reference to Jesus by Christians, however, the prophecy of the Messiah long predated the time of Jesus. Therefore, it does not indicate the work of a Christian editor, but simply that the youths believed a Messiah would come to save the Judeans. This story could also be interpreted as evidence that Judas the hammer was once considered the Messiah, as he drove the Greeks out of Judea. However, he is not viewed that way today. If the story was associated with Judas' cause at one point, it could explain why 6th and 8th Maccabees refer to the youths as the Maccabean martyrs.

The name of the lady is also rendered strangely in 7th Maccabees. In 6th Maccabees, she is called Lady Shamoni (ܫܡܘܢܝ ܡܪܬܐ), however, in 7th Maccabees the term mrtå (ܡܪܬܐ) is sometimes spelled as mrîm (מרים) or mrtîm (מרתים). Mrtå (ܡܪܬܐ / מרתא) was the Syriac word for 'lady' or 'noble woman,' which was adopted as the name Martha (Μάρθα) in Greek, and spread into most European languages. As a result, her name is sometimes translated as 'Martha,' with both mrîm and mrtîm dismissed as scribal errors. Nevertheless, mrtîm (מרתים) was the Judeo-Aramaic word for 'ladies,' suggesting the word is not an error but a transliteration from an older source text. The Syriac form of Aramaic used simpler pluralization, and mrtå (ܡܪܬܐ) was both the singular and plural form of the word 'lady/ladies.' Therefore, the terms mrtîm (מרתים) or mrtå (ܡܪܬܐ) are both translated as the title 'lady' in this translation.

It is unclear why the term would have been pluralized in the original Judeo-Aramaic text unless there were originally more than one lady in the text. It suggests her original name was Mary Shamone (מרים שמונה), however, this name is not consistent with Judean or Aramaic naming conventions from the era. If Mary was a mistranslation of mrtîm (מרתים), then this likely originated as a reference to eight noble women, not one. If so, the original title of this work was *The Story of the Ladies and Their Seven Sons.*

In 563 AD, a Syrian scholar named John Malálas (Ἰωάννης Μαλάλας / ܝܘܚܢܢ ܡܠܠܐ) composed a history of the world subsequently called the Chronographia (Χρονογραφία). The Chronographia was written in Greek, however, John was drawing from both Greek and Syriac sources and created one of the longer historical works of the era. His Chronographia was later translated into several ancient languages, and fragments survive in Georgian and Old Slavonic. It was eighteen volumes long, however, is of limited historical value, as it combines ancient mythologies, biblical stories, and events copied from older historical texts into a fantastical history of the world.

Some of the earlier historians that John drew on are accepted as the Greek writers Eusebius of Caesarea and Eustathius of Epiphania, however, his Syriac sources are undocumented. John's work is unusual for the era as he was focused on creating a work for monks and commoners, not the aristocrats. This is likely why it was carried to as many lands as it was and used as a source by later authors. One of the major works to use it as a source is the Primary Chronicle, one of the earliest Eastern Slavic works, believed to have been compiled near Kyiv in the 1110s. John's literary style was simple, reflecting the straightforward communication of the written language of everyday business of the era.

The majority of the Chronographia focused on the history of Antioch and then Constantinople, which is believed to have reflected John's move from Antioch to Constantinople in 540, caused by the Persians attacking Antioch. Based on his diction, he is believed to have been a lawyer, however, some have theorized he was a religious scholar. A very small section of his work mentions the beginning of the Maccabean Revolt, which has garnered the attention of academics studying the era. His text is clearly influenced by the Syriac tradition here and ignores the Greek entirely for some reason. He referred to the seven martyrs Antiochus Epiphanes killed as the Maccabees, the same as the Syriac poem *Lady Shamoni and the Maccabean Martyrs*, which Western biblical scholars have dubbed 6th Maccabees. None of the Greek, Hebrew, or Arabic translations refer to the martyrs as the Maccabean martyrs. This section of the Chronographia has been dubbed 8th Maccabees by scholars studying Maccabean literature.

Peshitta 5th Maccabees: Chapter 1

The miseries grew worse, and the Romans assaulted the tower of Antonia.

The misery of Jerusalem worsened daily, and the rebels grew more agitated by the calamities, as the famine ravaged them, as it had previously ravaged the people. Multitudes of bodies lay in heaps, one upon another, creating a horrible sight. They produced an infectious stench, which hindered those who wanted to make forays out of the city to fight the enemy.

However, those who had gone out in battle formation, who were already used to slaughtered legions, walked on those dead bodies as they marched. They were not terrified, nor did they pity the men they marched over. They did not see this as an insult to the dead, to bring any ill omen upon themselves, as they had already polluted their right hands with the murders of their countrymen, and so ran out to fight with foreigners. They seem to me to have cast a reproach upon God[1] himself, as he was too slow to punish them. The war was not going in a way that indicated they had any hope of victory, and they gloried in their savagery as they did not believe their salvation would be coming.

The Romans, even though they struggled greatly to gather enough material, managed to raise their siege mounds in twenty-one days. They had cut down all the trees that were in the land around the city, and for ninety stadions[2] around it, as I have already stated. The land looked terrible and was depressing because those places that were previously adorned with trees and pleasant gardens had become desolate in every way as the trees had all been cut down. Any foreigner who had seen Judea before, and the beautiful suburbs of the city, but now saw it as a wasteland lamented and mourned sadly at such a great change, as the war had destroyed all signs of beauty. If anyone that had known the place before, returned suddenly now, he wouldn't have recognized it. Even if he was in the city itself, he would ask where it was in disbelief.

When the siege mounds were finished, they brought a sense of trepidation to both the Romans and the Judeans. The Judeans expected that the city would be captured if they didn't burn the siege mounds. The Romans were expecting this, and knew if they were burned down once, they would never be able to capture it, because materials were scarce. The soldiers' bodies began to fail under such hard labor, and their minds fainted because they had failed so many times. The troubles in the city were a greater discouragement to the Romans than to those within the city, as they found the Judean soldiers to not be disheartened at all by their afflictions, while they themselves had less and less hopes of success.

Their siege mounds were damaged by the strategies of the enemy, their war machines to the firmness of the wall, and their closest attacks to the boldness of the counter-attack. Their greatest discouragement of all was that they found the Judeans' courageous minds to overcome the many miseries they were enduring, caused by their rebellion, their famine, and the war itself. They were ready to imagine that the violence of their counterattacks was invincible, and their eagerness would not be discouraged by their problems, as what wouldn't they be able to do if they were to become victorious? They had already used their misfortunes to improve their bravery! These considerations made the Romans keep a stronger guard around their siege mounds than they had before.

John and his militia were cautious in their attempt to capture it, in case the wall should be breached and fell to an assault before battering rams were brought against them. They did not achieve in the attempt, as they had gone out with their torches. They returned greatly discouraged before they had approached the siege mounds, as their actions did not seem to be unanimous, but they went out in distinct groups, at distinct intervals, and in a slow manner, and cautiously, and to put simply, without Judean courage.

They had become defective in what is peculiar to our nation, that is, in the boldness of violent assault, in charging the enemy altogether, and in continuing on their intent even though they do not at first succeed in it. They went out in a more unenthusiastic manner than usual and found the Romans set in formation, and more courageous than ordinary.

The armored guards protecting the siege mound surrounded it with their bodies so densely that there was no room to carry a fire between them. Every one of their minds was so courageous, that they would sooner die than desert their ranks, as they believed they would have no chance if the siege-mound was burnt down. The soldiers were embarrassed that their tactics were defeated by courage, their madness by armor, and their numbers by skill, the Judeans by the Romans.

The Romans also had another advantage, as their artillery accurately shot arrows and threw boulders from a distance at the Judeans when they were exiting the city. When a man fell he became an impediment to the one who followed him, and the danger of going farther made them less zealous in their attempts. For those who had run under the arrows, some of them were terrified by the good order and closeness of the enemies' ranks as they approached to fight, while others were speared with their lances, and retreated. Eventually, they insulted one another for their cowardice and retreated without accomplishing anything. This attack was made on the first day of the month of Panamos.[3]

When the Judeans retreated the Romans brought their war machines forward, even though they were under assault of boulders hurled at them from the tower of Antonia. They were also attacked by fire and sword, and by all sorts of arrows the Judeans had, because, although they had great faith in their wall and a contempt for the Roman battering rams, they still tried to stop the Romans from bringing them close. The Romans who struggled to bring the battering rams, thought that this zeal of the Judeans was to avoid any damage being made to the tower of Antonia. They assumed its wall was weak and its foundations decayed.

The tower did not yield to the blows from the battering ram, yet the Romans did feel the impact of their enemies' arrows which were constantly shot at them. They did not turn back from any of those dangers that fell on them from above, and they brought their war machines forward. However, as they approached the wall, they were savagely wounded by the stones dropped down on them, and some of them raised their shields above their bodies. Partly with their hands with the strength of their bodies, and partly with prybars, they undermined the foundations, and with great struggle, they removed four of its stones. When night fell the attack ended, however, the wall had been so damaged by the battering rams in the area where John had prepared his strategy, that the foundations were damaged, and the ground excavated causing the wall to suddenly collapse.

When this collapse unexpectedly happened, the minds of both parties were affected. One would expect that the Judeans would be discouraged, because this fall of their wall was unexpected, and they had made no provision for it, however, they were encouraged because the tower of Antonia was still standing.

The sudden exuberance of the Romans, when the wall fell, was quickly shattered by the sight of another wall that John and his militia had built within the outer walls. The second wall appeared to be much weaker than the first, however, it was more difficult to approach through the collapsed parts of the outer wall. The new wall appeared to be much weaker than the tower of Antonia, and so the Romans believed that it had been erected quickly, and they could quickly pull it down, yet no one would approach this wall, as whoever did, would certainly die.

Titus contemplated that the enthusiasm of soldiers at war was mainly excited by hopes and by good words and that exhortations and promises frequently make men forget the hazards they encounter, and sometimes they even mock death itself.

He gathered the most courageous of his army and tried to inspire his men stating, "Fellow soldiers, to exhort men to do what is not dangerous, is not very glorious to those whom the exhortation is made. Indeed, for he who makes the exhortation, it is a sign of his own cowardice as well. Therefore, I think that such exhortations should only be made when missions are dangerous, and yet are worthy of being attempted."

"I completely agree with you that it is a difficult task to approach this wall, but it is proper for those who desire a reputation for their valor to struggle with difficulties when they appear. I have specifically stated that it is a brave thing to die with glory, and that courage here necessary will not go unrewarded for those who first begin the attempt. Let my first argument move you to abandon what some would probably think reasonable, I mean the commitment and patience of these Judeans even under their ill successes. It is unbecoming of you, who are Romans and my soldiers, who have been taught how to make wars during peacetime, and who are used to conquering in wars, to be inferior to Judeans, either in the action of your hands or in the courage of your minds. This is especially when you are near the conclusion of your victory and are assisted by the gods themselves."

"Our misfortunes have because of the madness of the Judeans, while their suffering has been caused by your valor, and to the assistance the gods have given you. As to the rebellion they have fought, the famine they suffer, the siege they now endure, and the fall of their walls without our battering rams, what can they all be other than demonstrations of the gods' anger against them, and of their assistance to us? Therefore, it is not right for you to either show yourselves inferior to those who you are really superior to or to betray that divine assistance which is offered you."

"Indeed, how can it be considered any other way than an immoral and unworthy thing, that while the Judeans, who do not need be ashamed if they are abandoned because they have long ago learned to be slaves to others, yet still despise death so much that they may no longer exist. Still, they frequently make sorties into the very midst of us with no hopes of conquering us, but merely to demonstrate their courage. We, who have conquered most of the world by either land or sea and for whom it will be a great dishonor if we fail to conquer them, do not once even attempt to attack our enemies when there is a great deal of danger?"

"We still sit idle, with the brave armies we have, and only wait for famine and fortune to conclude our business? This, when we have it within our power, with some small danger, to gain all that we desire? If we go up to this tower of Antonia, we'll capture the city. If there is any more fighting against those in the city, which I doubt there will be, we will then have the high ground and be on our enemies before they can take a breath. These advantages promise no less than a certain and sudden victory. As for myself, I will now wave any commendation of those who die in battle, and never speak of the immortality of those men who are killed during their brave combat."

"However, I cannot avoid cursing those who have an opposite disposition. Those who may die in peacetime through some political disorder or other, since their spirits are condemned to the grave, together with their bodies. For what man of virtue is there who doesn't know that those spirits who are severed from their fleshly bodies in battles by the sword are received by the ether, that purest of elements, and joined to the armies that are placed among the stars? They become good demons, and fortunate heroes, and reveal themselves to their posterity afterwards."

"While those spirits who fade away in and with their discomposing bodies, come to nothing in a subterranean night, dissolve, and a deep oblivion takes away all memory of them. Nevertheless, they become clean from all blemishes and defilements of this world, so that, in this way, the spirit also comes to the end of its life, its body, and its memorial. But since he has decided it, Mot⁴ will come to all men, and a sword is a better tool for that purpose than any disease. So why isn't it a very minor thing for us to give up to the public good that which we must surrender to fate?"

"This argument I have made is predicated on the assumption that those who first attempt to capture this wall will be killed in the attempt, yet men of true courage still have a chance to survive even in the most dangerous missions. First of all, the part of the former wall that has collapsed is easily captured, and the newly built wall is easily destroyed. Therefore, you, many of you, become courageous and set about this work. Mutually encourage and help one another, and your bravery will soon break the spirits of your enemies."

"Perhaps this glorious undertaking of yours may be accomplished without bloodshed. It's fair to expect the Judeans will try to stop you when you begin to attack them. However, when you have protected yourselves from them, and driven them back with force. They will not be able to sustain a defense against you any longer even if only a few of you defend yourselves against them and get over the wall. As for the person who first mounts the wall, I would blush in shame if I did not make him the envied of all others through the rewards I will heap upon him. If he survives with his life, he shall have the command of others who are now his equals, although it is also true that the greatest rewards will be given to those who die in the attempt."

After this speech of Titus, the rest of the group was terrified at such great danger, but there was one whose name was Sabinus, a soldier who served among the cohort, a Syrian by birth. He was renowned for his great strength both from his actions and the courage of his spirit. Before he began his work, anyone would have thought his body was too weak, and that he was not fit to be a soldier. His color was black, and his body was lean and thin, but there was a certain heroic spirit that lived in this small body, a body that was indeed much too thin for the amount of courage within him. Therefore he was the first who rose up, and said, "I readily surrender myself to you, Caesar! I will be first to ascend the wall, and I wish that my fortune may follow my courage and my resolution. If some terrible fate begrudges me the success of my attack, take notice that my failure to succeed is not unexpected, but that I choose death voluntarily for your sake."

After he said this, he lifted his shield over his head with his left hand, and with his sword in his right hand, marched up to the wall around the sixth hour of the day. Only eleven others followed him, who had decided to imitate his bravery, but nevertheless, he was the leader of them all and went first excited by a divine fury. Those who guarded the wall shot at them from there and shot uncountable arrows at them from every side. They also dropped boulders onto them, which killed some of those eleven that were with him. As for Sabinus himself, he met the arrows that were shot at him and though he was overwhelmed with them, he did not stop his assault before he had reached the top of the wall and had caused the enemy to flee.

The Judeans were astonished at his great strength and the bravery of his spirit. They also thought more of them had climbed up the wall than really had, so they ran. One cannot but complain here of Fortune still being envious of Virtue, and always hindering the performance of great achievements, as this is what happened to the man in front of us. When he had just obtained his goal, he tripped on a large stone and fell down face first, making a great noise. The Judeans turned back, and when they saw him alone and fallen down, they shot their arrows into him from all directions.

However, he got up to his knee and covered himself with his shield. At first, he could defend himself against them and wounded many of those who approached him, but he was soon forced to relax his right hand because of the number of wounds that had been inflicted upon him, until, eventually, he was filled with arrows and he gave up his spirit. He deserved a better fate due to his bravery, but, as might be expected, he fell under such a great onslaught. As for the rest of his party, the Judeans dashed three of them to pieces with boulders as they were climbing up the wall, and the other eight were wounded and knocked down, and carried back to the camp. This happened on the third day of the month of Panemus.

Two days afterward, twelve of the men who were at the front keeping watch on the siege mounds, got together and called to them the standard-bearer of the fifth legion, two of the cavalrymen, and one trumpeter. These traveled quietly around the ninth hour of the night, through the rubble to the tower of Antonia.

The first guards they encountered were asleep, and so they cut their throats, and then took possession of the wall, and ordered the trumpeter to sound his trumpet. The rest of the guards suddenly woke up and ran away, before anybody could see how many of them had climbed up. They were running both from fear and confusion from the sound of the trumpet that they heard, they imagined many of the enemy had climbed up.

As soon as Caesar heard the signal, he ordered the army to immediately put on their armor and approached with his commanders. He ascended first of all with the chosen men he took with him. As the Judeans were retreating to the temple, the Romans fell into the pit that John had dug. Then the rebelling Judean militias, both that belonging to John, as well as that belonging to Simon, attacked them. They did not hold back the highest degree of brutality and enthusiasm, as they knew they would be entirely ruined if the Romans got into the temple.

The Romans also had this belief since the beginning of their conquest, so a terrible battle was fought at the entrance of the temple. The Romans were trying to force their way in to capture the temple, but the Judeans were driving them back towards the tower of Antonia. In this battle, arrows were useless on both sides, as were spears, and both sides drew their swords and fought hand to hand. During this struggle, the positions of the men were unclear on both sides, and they fought randomly, the men being mixed with each other, and confused because of the narrowness of the place. The noise that was heard was indistinct because it was so very loud.

There was a great slaughter on both sides, and the combatants trod on the bodies and the armor of those who were dead and crushed them to pieces. Whenever the battle advanced one way or the other, those who had the advantage urged one another to go on, while the beaten made great lamentation. There was no room to withdraw or to pursue, but disorderly turnabouts and retreats, while the armies were mixed with one another. Those who were in the first ranks needed to kill or be killed, without any hope of escaping. Those on both sides who came behind forced those before them to go on, without leaving any space between the armies.

At length, the Judeans' violent zeal was too much for the Romans' skill. The battle turned their way as the fighting had lasted from the ninth hour of the night until the seventh hour of the day. The Judeans advanced in crowds, motivated by the danger to the temple, while the Romans had only a part of their army. Those legions, on which their soldiers depended could not advance to them. Therefore, it was decided by the Romans that the capture of the tower of Antonia was enough.

There was one centurion named Julian who came from Bithynia, a man of great reputation whom I had formerly encountered in that war, and one of the highest fame, for his skill in battle, strength of body, and the courage of his mind. When this man saw the

Romans being pushed back, and not happy about it as he stood with Titus at the tower of Antonia, leaped out and by himself alone caused the Judeans to flee. When they had almost been conquerors, he made them fall back as far as the corner of the inner court of the temple. The multitude fled away from him in crowds believing that neither his strength nor his brutality could be those of a mortal man. Therefore, he rushed through the middle of the Judeans as they fled in all directions, and killed those that he caught.

There was no sight more wonderful in the eyes of Caesar, or more terrible to the others, than this. However, he was himself pursued by a fate which it all possible for him, who was but a mortal man, to escape. He had sandals with thick sharp hobnails, as had all the other soldiers, and when he ran on the pavement of the temple, he slipped and fell down, landing on his back with a very great noise caused by his armor. Those that were running away heard it and turned back. The Romans in the tower of Antonia shouted out loudly, as they were afraid for the man.

The Judeans surrounded him in crowds and stabbed him with their spears and swords from all sides. He blocked a great many wounds from these iron weapons with his shield, and repeatedly attempted to get up again, but was knocked down by those who struck at him. He countered this and killed many of them with his sword. He was not killed quickly, as he was protected by his helmet and breastplate in all parts of his body where he might be mortally wounded. He also pulled his neck close to his body, until all his other limbs were shattered. Nobody came to defend him, and he fell to his fate.

Caesar was deeply affected because of this man's great fortitude, especially as he was killed in the sight of so many people. He wanted to help him himself, but the place would not allow him, and those who could have done it were too terrified to try. When Julian had struggled with death for a long time, and had only a few of those who had given him his mortal wound escape uninjured, he at last had his throat cut, though not without some difficulty, and left behind great fame not only among the Romans, including Caesar himself, but among his enemies also.

Then the Judeans passed over his dead body, and caused the Romans to fall back again, and trapped them in the tower of Antonia. Those who most distinguished themselves, and fought most zealously in this battle on the Judean side were Alexas and Gyphtheus from John's militia, and from Simon's militia were Malachi, Judas the son of Merto, and James the son of Sosas, the commander of the Edomites. From the zealots were two brothers: Simon and Judas, the sons of Jairus.

Peshitta 5th Maccabees: Chapter 1 Notes

1 Syriac: dålhn (ܕܐܠܗܢ). Translation: the god

The term ålhn (ܐܠܗܢ) is used in the Peshitta's Old Testament as a transliteration for the Hebrew word elohim (אֱלֹהִים), however, can also be interpreted as 'gods' in Judeo-Aramaic. The Hebrew word is also a plural form, however, is generally accepted as referring to the specific god Yhwh by the Classical era, and so is translated as 'God' by both Christians and Jews. Nevertheless, Josephus is believed to have written his books in Judeo-Aramaic, in which dålhn (דאלהן) could be translated as 'the gods' when referring to foreign gods, or 'the God,' when referring to the Jewish God. Therefore, this term is translated as either 'God' or 'the gods,' depending on the context.

2 Syriac: åṣṭdůtå (ܐܣܛܕܘܬܐ). Translation: stadion (or stadion)

The stadion (στάδιον) was a Greek measurement of distance roughly equal to 185.4 meters.

3 The month of Pánamos (Πάναμος) on the Macedonian calender was approximately at the same time as the Gregorian month of June.

4 Syriac: mûtå (ܪܬܘܡ). Translation: death (or Mot)

Mot was the Canaanite god of death, and word meaning 'death,' spelled variously as mâtum (ܪ—), mt (ܠ—), and mût (ܬܘܡ). He was interpreted as the messenger of death by the Classical Jews and early Christians, translated into Syriac as mûtå (ܪܬܘܡ) and Greek as Thanatos (Θάνατος). As Josephus refers to death as making a decision in this verse, it is clear he was referring to the god or messenger. In the original Greek, this would have been interpreted as a reference to the god Thanatos, however, the Christian translation of the book could also be interptered as a reference to the messenger of death, assuming the decision maker in the sentence was interpreted as God. Of course, as Titus was not a Jew or Christian, this interpretation would be anachronistic, and therefore the name Mot is used.

Peshitta 5th Maccabees: Chapter 2

How Titus gave orders to demolish the tower of Antonia and then persuaded Josephus to again encourage the Judeans to surrender.

Titus gave orders to his soldiers to dig up the foundations of the tower of Antonia and prepare a passage for his formation to enter. He had Josephus brought to himself, as he had been informed on that very day, which was the seventeenth day of Panamos, that the Korban sacrifice had not happened, and had not been offered to God, as there were no men to offer it, and that the people were deeply concerned about it.

He commanded him to say the same things to John that he had said before, that if he had any inclination for fighting, he could come out with as many of his men as he pleased and fight without the danger of destroying either his city or temple. If he desired it, he would not have defiled the temple, nor offended God. That he might, if he wanted, offer the sacrifices which had been missed, for any of the Judeans who were fighting at his side.

After hearing this, Josephus stood in a place where he would be heard, not just by John, but by many others, and declared what Caesar had told him to say, but in the Hebrew language. So he earnestly begged them to spare their own city and to prevent the fire which was just ready to engulf the temple and to offer their usual sacrifices to God within it. When he said these words, a great solemn silence was heard among the people. The tyrant himself, yelled many insults at Josephus, along with curses, and ended with the statement that he was not afraid of the city being captured because it was God's own city.

Josephus yelled back, "Have you kept this city wonderfully pure for the sake of God? Does the temple continue entirely unpolluted? Have you not been guilty of any ungodliness before He who you seek assistance? Does He still receive his ritual sacrifices? Vile wretch that you are, if anyone should deprive you of your daily bread, you would judge him to be an enemy of yours, yet you hope to have God as your ally in this war when you have deprived him of his eternal worship!"

"You blame this sin on the Romans, who continue to be careful to respect our laws, and almost compel these sacrifices to be still offered to God, which have through your hands been stopped! Who is here who can avoid groans and lamentations at the amazing change that has happened in this city? The foreigners and enemies now correct the disrespect that you have caused, while you, who is Jewish, and was educated in our laws, have become a greater enemy to us than the others."

"Nevertheless, John, it is never dishonorable to repent and correct what has been done incorrectly, even the worst possible things. There is the example of Jeconiah, the king of the Judahites, if you want to save the city. When the king of Babylon made war against him, he chose to go out of this city before it was captured, and surrendered into captivity with his family so that the sanctuary might not be conquered by the enemy, and that he might not see the Temple of God set on fire. Because of this, he is celebrated among all the Judeans in their sacred memorials, and his memory has become immortal, and will be repeated down to our descendants through all ages."

"This, John, is an excellent example of a similar time of danger, and I dare to promise that the Romans will still forgive you. Take note that I, who am advising you, am one of your own nation. I am a Judean and making this promise to you. It would be wise for you to consider who I am, who gives you this advice, and where I come from. As long as I am alive, I shall never be a slave, or allow my own king to be, or forget the laws of our forefathers."

"You are angry at me again and yell at me, and insult me. I cannot deny that I deserve this treatment and worse, because, in opposition to fate, I make this kind invitation to you, and am trying to force deliverance on those who God has condemned. Who is there who does not know what the writings of the ancient prophets contain in them? Particularly that oracle which is just now being fulfilled upon this miserable city? They predicted that this city would be captured when somebody began the slaughter of his own countrymen. Are not both the city and the temple entirely filled with the dead bodies of your countrymen? It is God, therefore, it is God himself who is bringing on this fire to purge the city and temple using the Romans, and is going to reap this city, which is full of your pollution."

As Josephus spoke these words, with moaning, and tears in his eyes, his voice was broken by sobs. The Romans felt pity for the pain he was under and marveled at his actions. John and those who were with him were even more confused by the Romans because of this and wanted to get Josephus onto their side. His discourse influenced many of the better type, and truly some of them were so afraid of the guards set by the rebels that they stayed where they were, but believed that both they and the city were doomed to destruction.

Some had been quietly waiting for a good opportunity when they might quietly escape, and fled to the Romans. They included the high priests Joseph and Jesus, the three sons of high priests Ishmael who was beheaded in Cyrene, and the four sons of Matthias the son of Matthias who ran away after his father's death, and whose father was killed by Simon the son of Gioras, with his three sons, as I have already stated. Many of the other nobility also went over to the Romans, together with the high priests.

Caesar not only welcomed these men kindly, but, knowing they would not willingly live following the customs of other nations, he sent them to Gophna, and asked them to remain there for a while. He told them that when the war was over, he would restore each of them to their possessions again, so they cheerfully traveled to that small city that was provided to them, without fear of danger.

But as they were not to be found, the rebels said that these were deserters who were killed by the Romans. They said this to deter the rest from running away, for fear of similar treatment. This trick of theirs succeeded for a while, as did a similar trick before, and the rest were deterred from deserting, for fear of similar treatment.

Titus recalled those men from Gophna and ordered them to circle the wall with Josephus and show themselves to the people, and then a great many more fled to the Romans. These men amassed in great numbers, and stood before the Romans begging the rebels with groans and tears in their eyes, firstly to allow the Romans to enter the city and save their own home, but if they would not agree to this, they would at least retreat from the temple, and save the sacred temple for its own use, as the Romans would not set the sanctuary on fire except as a last resort.

Yet the rebels still continued to argue with them, and while they yelled louder and more terrible insults at these deserters, they also prepared their machines for shooting arrows, javelins, and boulders from the sacred gates of the temple. They were spread out evenly, covering the space all around the temple so that assaulting would become like a burial ground, as the holy temple itself could be compared to a citadel.

These men rushed into these holy places in their armor which was otherwise inaccessible, and while their hands were still warm with the blood of their own people which they had killed. They committed such great transgressions that the very same indignation which Judeans would naturally have against Romans they had been guilty of, such abuses against them, the Romans now had against Judeans, for their impiety regarding their own religious customs. Indeed, there were none of the Roman soldiers who did not look with a sacred horror upon the holy temple, and adore it, and wished that the rebels would repent before their miseries became incurable.

Titus was deeply affected by this state of things, insulted John and his militia, and said to them, "Haven't you vile wretches that you are, by our permission, erected this barrier around your sanctuary? Have not you been allowed to put up the signs around it at due distances engraved in Greek and your own letters which prohibited foreigners from entering the barrier? Have we not permitted you to kill any who goes beyond it, even if he was a Roman? What do you do now, you evil villains? Why do you trample upon dead bodies in this temple? Why do you pollute this sacred temple with the blood of both foreigners and Judeans themselves? I appeal to the gods of my own country, and to every god that ever had any regard for this place, for I do not suppose it to be now regarded by any of them. I also appeal to my own army, and to those Judeans that are now with me, and even to yourselves, that I do not force you to defile your sanctuary! If you will just change the place where you fight, no Roman will enter your sanctuary, or attack it. I will endeavor to preserve you your sacred temple, whether you will or not."

Josephus interpreted these things from the mouth of Caesar, both the rebels and the tyrant thought that this council came from Titus's fear, and not from his goodwill to them, and grew insolent after hearing it. When Titus saw that these men were neither to be moved by pity towards themselves nor had any concern for saving the sacred temple, he resigned to continue the war against them. He could not bring all of his army against them as the place was so narrow, but chose thirty of the most valiant soldiers out of every hundred, and committed a thousand to each tribune. He made Cerealis their commander-in-chief, and he gave orders that they should attack the guards of the temple at the ninth hour of that night.

He dressed in his armor and prepared to go down with them, but his friends would not let him go because of the great danger, and what the commanders suggested to them. They advised that he would do more by sitting high in the tower of Antonia, giving rewards to those soldiers that distinguished themselves in the fight, than by coming down and endangering his own body in the vanguard, as they would all fight better while Caesar watched them.

Caesar followed this advice and said his only reason for such compliance with the soldiers was that he might be able to judge their courageous actions and that no valiant soldier might remain unknown and miss his reward, and no cowardly soldier might go unpunished. He could himself be an eye-witness, and able to give evidence of all that was done, he who was the disposer of punishments and rewards for them. He sent the soldiers about at the arranged hour, while he went up to a higher place in the tower of Antonia, where he could see what was done, and waited there impatiently to see the event.

The soldiers that were sent did not find the guards at the temple asleep, as they hoped, but were forced to fight with them immediately in hand-to-hand combat, as they rushed violently at them with a great shout. As soon as the others within the temple heard that shout of those who were on watch, they ran out in squads at them.

The Romans fought the first troops that approached them, but those who followed them attacked their own troops, and many of them treated their own soldiers as if they were enemies. There was a great confusion of noise that was made on both sides, which stopped them from distinguishing one another's voices. Also, the darkness of the night hindered them from determining who their enemies were, and the blindness that arose from the passion and the fear they were in at the same time. For all these reasons, it was not clear who the soldiers were who they were killing. However, this confusion affected the Romans less than the Judeans, because they were joined together under their shields, and made their attacks more regularly than the others did. Each of them also remembered their watch-word, while the Judeans were constantly spread around, and made their attacks and retreats at random, and so frequently mistook each other to be enemies. Every one of them fought those of their own men who came back in the dark, confusing them for Romans assaulting them.

More of them were wounded by their own men than by the enemy until the break of day, and what was happening became visible. Then they stood in battle formation in distinct groups, and shot their arrows regularly, and defended themselves properly. However, neither side yielded or grew weary. The Romans competed with each other over who could fight the most strenuously, both single men and entire regiments, as they were under the eye of Titus. Everyone believed that this day would begin his advancement if he fought bravely.

The greatest encouragement for the Judeans to act vigorously was their fear for themselves and for the temple, along with the presence of their tyrant, who encouraged some to act courageously while beating and threatening others. This fight was mostly a stationary one, wherein the soldiers attacked and retreated quickly and suddenly, for there wasn't much territory for either of their flights or pursuits. Still, there was a great noise among the Romans from the tower of Antonia, who loudly shouted out whenever their own men advanced courageously, or when they were too hard for the Judeans, but quiet when they were retreating backward. It became a kind of theater of war, for what was done in this fight could not be hidden either from Titus or from those who were around him.

This fight that had begun in the ninth hour of the night, was not over until after the fifth hour of the day, and yet, was in the same place where the battle had begun, as neither party could make the other retreat. The victory was uncertain between the armies, however, those who distinguished themselves on the Roman side were many, but on the Judean side, and of those who were with Simon, Judas the son of Merto, and Simon the son of Josas. From the Edomites were James and Simon the son of Cathlas, and James the son of Sosas. From those who were with John: Gyphtheus and Alexas, and of the zealots: Simon the son of Jairus.

Over the following seven days, the rest of the Roman army destroyed some foundations of the tower of Antonia and broadened and road to the temple. When the legions approached the outer court and began to raise siege banks. One siege mount was near the northwest corner of the outer temple, and another was at that northern edifice which was between the two gates, the third one was at the western colonnade of the outer court of the temple, and the fourth was against its northern colonnade. However, these works were built by the Romans with great difficulty, being forced to bring their materials from a distance of a hundred stadions.

They had additional difficulties as well, sometimes by the extreme security they were in, so they would not be killed by Judean traps set for them, and by that boldness of the Judeans who had been inspired by their desire to escape. Some of their horsemen, when they went out to gather wood or hay, let their horses feed without having their bridles on, which whole groups of Judeans would raid and capture. When this happened repeatedly, Caesar believed that the horses were stolen more by the negligence of his own men than by the valor of the Judeans, and he decided to use greater severity to oblige the rest to take care of their horses. He commanded that one of those soldiers who had lost their horses should be capitally punished, which so terrified the rest that they preserved their horses for a later time, and they did not allow them to leave them to feed, but, as if they had raised them, they went always along with them when they fed.

The Romans continued to wage war against the temple and to raise their siege mounds against it. On the day after the Romans had broken through the wall, many of the rebels were so hungry and depressed by the failure of their attacks, that they got together, and assaulted the Roman guards that were on the Mount of Olives. This was about the eleventh hour of the day, as they supposed that they would not expect such an attack, and also they were bathing at the time, and therefore they should have easily defeated them. However, the Romans were told about their attack beforehand, and quickly assembled together from the neighboring camps. They prevented them from getting over their walls or breaking through the wall that was built around them.

It was a vicious fight with many great acts on both sides. The Romans showed both their courage and their skill in war, as the Judeans came at them with excessive violence and intolerable passion. The one group was urged on by shame, and the other by necessity. It seemed very shameful to the Romans to let the Judeans go, now that they were captured as if in a net. While the Judeans had only one hope of saving themselves, and that was if they could violently break through the Roman wall.

A cavalryman named Pedanius chased the Judeans as they fell back down into the valley, spurred his horse on their flank with great fury, and caught a certain young man by his ankle as he was running away. However, this man was large and was wearing heavy armor. Pedanius bent himself down so low from his horse as he was galloping, and the strength of his right arms so great, along with the rest of his body, and he was so skilled at horsemanship, that this man grabbed his prey like a precious treasure, and carried him as his captive to Caesar.

Titus admired the man who had seized the other for his great strength and ordered the man who had been caught to be punished for his attack on the Roman wall. Then he traveled to the siege of the temple, and to order the raising of the siege walls.

The Judeans were so distressed by the fights they had been in, as the war advanced higher and higher, creeping up towards the sacred temple itself, that they, as it were, cut off those limbs of their body that were infected to prevent the disease from spreading further. They set the northwest colonnade on fire, which was connected to the tower of Antonia. Between that colonnade and the sanctuary was a gap of around twelve cubits, so they had begun burning it to isolate the sanctuary. Two days later, which was the twenty-fourth day of the month of Panamos (or Tammuz),[1] the Romans set fire to the next colonnade, and the fire went fifteen cubits farther.

The Judeans, in turn, cut off its roof. They completely stopped what they were doing until the tower of Antonia was severed from the temple. Even when they could have stopped the fire they did not. They remained still even when the temple was first set on fire, as they saw this spreading of the fire to be to their advantage. However, the armies were still fighting one another around the temple, and the war was a series of continuous assaults of small groups against one another.

There was at this time a short man among the Judeans, of a despicable appearance. His name was Jonathan, but he was of no account, either by his family or in any other respect. He went out to the high priest John's camp and shouted insults at the Romans, and challenged the best of them all to a single combat. Many of those who stood there in the army dismissed him, but many of them were afraid of him. Some of them also reasoned justly enough that it was not right to fight with a man who desired to die because those who had no hope of survival, and passionately wanted violence by attacking men that could not be defeated, had no regard for the gods themselves. Additionally, to risk oneself with a person that, if you defeat, you don't accomplish anything great, yet through whom you risk being taken prisoner, would not be an example of manly courage, but of unmanly recklessness.

Therefore nobody came out to accept the man's challenge, and the Judean dishonored them with a great number of insults, calling them cowards, as he was a very haughty man and one who hated the Romans. A cavalryman named Pudens, prompted by his disgust of the other's words and of his impudence, and perhaps out of an inconsiderate arrogance on account of the other's short stature, ran out to him, and was too much for him in other respects, but was betrayed by his ill fortune. He tripped, and as he was down, Jonathan came running to him and cut his throat, and then, standing upon his dead body, he lifted his sword, bloody as it was, and shook his shield with his left hand, and made many acclamations to the Roman army, and exulted over the dead man, and joked about the Romans.

After some time, a centurion named Priscus, shot an arrow at him as he was leaping around and playing the fool, and pierced him through. A shout went out both by the Judeans and the Romans, though for different reasons. Jonathan grew giddy because of the pain of his wounds, and fell down onto the body of his enemy, as an example of how suddenly vengeance may come on men who have success in war, without justly deserving it.

Peshitta 5ᵗʰ Maccabees: Chapter 2 Notes

1 Syriac: tmůz (ܬܡܘܙ). Translation: Tammuz

Tammuz (תַּמּוּז / تموز / ܬܡܘܙ / Temmuz) is a month on the Jewish ecclesiastical calendar, along with the calendars used in Iraq, Syria, Lebanon, and Turkey, which roughly corresponds with late June and early July. It is descended from the ancient Sumerian month of Dumuzid (𒌉𒍣𒉺). The month of Pánamos (Πάναμος) on the Macedonian calendar, which was mentioned in the verse, was approximately at the same time as the Gregorian month of June.

Peshitta 5th Maccabees: Chapter 3

Concerning a strategy that was devised by the Judeans, through which they burnt many of the Romans, with another description of the terrible famine that was in the city.

The rebels that were in the temple tried each day to beat back the soldiers that were on the siege mounds, and on the twenty-seventh day of the month conceived the following strategy. They filled the part of the western colonnade that was between the beams and the roof beneath them with dry materials, and also with bitumen and pitch, and then retreated from the place acting as though they were fatigued with the pains they had received.

This act of theirs caused many of the most thoughtless of the Romans, who were engulfed in violent passions to chase quickly after them as they were retreating, and raised ladders to the colonnade, and climbed up to it quickly. However, the wise among them, when they saw this unaccountable retreat of the Judeans, remained where they were. The colonnade filled with those who had gone up the ladders, and then the Judeans set it on fire. The flame instantly burst out all around them, and the Romans that were not in immediate danger were suddenly very concerned, while those that were in immediate danger were panicking. When they saw that they were surrounded by flames, some of them jumped back down into the city, and some towards their enemies. Many who jumped down to their own men broke their limbs to pieces. Many of those who were going up to attack were killed by the fire, although some were killed by their own swords.

However, the fire quickly spread and surrounded those who were about to die. As for Caesar, he could not do anything but commiserate those who died like this, although they had gone up there without any orders since there was no way to save any of them. Yet this was some comfort to those who were burned, that everyone might see that person grieve, for whose sake they came to their end. He cried out openly to them and leaped up, and ordered those who were around him to do their best to save them.

Every one of them died screaming, carrying along with him these words and this intention of Caesar as a sepulchral monument. Some had jumped within the wall of the colonnade, which was broad, and were saved from the fire, but were then surrounded by the Judeans. Although they fought the Judeans for a long time, they were wounded by them, and eventually, they all fell dead.

Near the end, a young man named Longus became worthy of being decorated in this sad affair. While every one of those who perished was worthy of a memorial, this man appeared to deserve it beyond all the rest. The Judeans admired this man for his courage but also wanted him killed, so they persuaded him to come down to them offering to spare his life. But his brother Cornelius persuaded him to do the opposite, and to not tarnish his own glory, nor that of the Roman army. He complied with this advice and lifted up his sword before both armies, and killed himself.

There was another surrounded by the fire, named Artorius, who escaped by his cunning. He called with a loud voice to Lucius, one of his fellow soldiers who bunked with him in the same tent, and said to him, "I will leave you as heir of all I have if you will come and save me." Upon hearing this, he came running quickly to save him, however, Artorius then jumped down upon him, and saved his own life, while he who was trying to save him was smashed so powerfully against the stone pavement by the other's weight, that he died immediately.

This sad accident made the Romans depressed for a while, but it also made them more on guard in the future. It was of advantage to them against the delusions of the Judeans, who had greatly damaged them through their ignorance of the place, and with the nature of the inhabitants.

This colonnade was burnt down as far as John's tower, which he built in the war he made against Simon above the gates that led to the portico. The Judeans also cut off the rest of that colonnade from the temple, after they had destroyed those who climbed up to it. The next day the Romans burnt down the northern colonnade entirely, as far as the east colonnade, whose common angle joined to the Valley of Cedron, and was built above it giving an awesome view. This was the state of the temple at that time.

The number of those who died by famine in the city was monstrous, and the misery they endured was indescribable. If even the shadow of any kind of food appeared anywhere, a fight immediately broke out, and the closest friends died fighting one another over it, snatching from each other the most miserable support of life. Men would not believe that those who were starving had no food, but thieves would search them when they were dying in case anyone had concealed food on their bodies and was pretending to be dying. These thieves found nothing, yet ran about stumbling and staggering like mad dogs and banging against the doors of the houses like drunks.

In the great distress, they were in, they would also rush into the same houses two or three times in the same day. Moreover, their hunger was so intolerable that it caused them to eat anything. They gathered things that even the lowest animals would not touch, and managed to eat them. They did not take long to start chewing girdles and shoes, and even the leather that belonged to their shields they pulled off and gnawed. Even very old straws of old hay became food for some, and some gathered up threads and sold even a very small amount of them for four Attican drachms.

So why do I describe the shameless foolishness that the famine brought on men, in their eating inanimate things? I am reporting exactly what happened, unlike every other history, either among the Greeks or Barbarians. It is horrible to tell it, and incredible when heard. If I willingly omitted this calamity of ours, I might not seem to deliver what this is. I have interviewed invaluable witnesses to it in my own era. Besides, my country would have had little reason to thank me for suppressing the misery that she underwent at this time.

There was a woman who lived beyond the Jordan named Mary the daughter of Eleazar, from the village of Bethezuba (which means the house of hyssop). She was known for her family and her wealth and had fled to Jerusalem with the rest of the multitude, and was besieged there with them. The property of this woman had been immediately stolen, I mean that which she had brought with her out of Perea when she moved to the city.

What she had stored up besides this, including the food that she had schemed to save, had been confiscated by the avaricious guards, who came into her house each day. This brought the poor woman into dire straights, and through the frequent insults she cast at these avaricious villains, she provoked them to anger against her, but none of them, either out of indignation or out of commiseration of her case, would kill her. If she found any food, she saw her labor was for others, and not for herself. Then it became impossible for them to find any more food, while the famine pierced her to the very bowels and marrow when also her anger was fired to a degree beyond the famine itself.

She thought of nothing but her anger and the situation she was in. She attempted a most unnatural thing, and grabbed her son, who was a babe sucking at her breast, and said, "You miserable infant! How will I save you in this war, this famine, and this rebellion? Regarding the war with the Romans, if they save our lives we will be slaves. This famine will destroy us, even before we become slaves. Yet these rebellious rogues are more terrible than the others. Come on, you'll be my food, and you'll be a malignancy to these rebellious scoundrels, and infamous in the world, and the only thing left to complete the calamities of us Judeans."

As soon as she said this, she killed her son and roasted him. She ate half of him and kept the other half hidden. The rebels came soon afterward, and when they smelled the pungent scent of this food. They threatened to cut her throat immediately if she did not show them what food she had prepared. She replied that she had saved a very fine piece of it for them, and uncovered what was left of her son. When they saw it they were filled with horror and stood amazed at the sight.

Then she said to them, "This is my son, and what has been done was my own doing! Come, eat this food, like I have eaten myself! Don't pretend to be either more tender than a woman or more compassionate than a mother. If you are so scrupulous, and hate my sacrifice, as I have eaten one half, let the rest be left for me also."

After this, those men left trembling, never being so afraid of anything as they were at this. With some difficulty, they left the rest of the body to the mother. Afterward, the whole city heard of this horrid event immediately, and when everyone considered this miserable case, they trembled as if this unheard-of action was something they would do themselves. Those who were distressed by the famine were very willing to die, and those already dead were considered fortunate because they had not lived long enough to either hear or see such misery.

This sad event was quickly told to the Romans, some of whom could not believe it, and others pitied the distress that the Judeans were under. Many of them were induced to a more bitter hatred than ordinary against our nation. But for Caesar, he excused himself before the gods regarding this matter and said that he had proposed peace and liberty to the Judeans, as well as expunging of all their former rebellious acts. Instead, they had chosen rebellion. Instead of peace, war. Instead of being satiated with abundance, a famine. "They had begun with their own hands to burn down the temple which we have preserved until now, and so they deserved to eat the little food that remained. However, this horrid act of eating one's own child ought to be the cause of the destruction of their country itself. Men ought not to leave a city like this on the habitable earth to be seen by the sun, where mothers are fed like this. Such food is fitter for the fathers than for the mothers to eat, since it is they who continued still in a state of war against us after they have undergone such misery as this."

At the same time that he said this, he reflected on the desperate condition these men must be in. He could not expect that such men could recover to sobriety of mind after they had endured this suffering, which was avoided if they had just repented.

Peshitta 5th Maccabees: Chapter 4

When the siege mounds were completed and the battering rams brought and could do nothing, Titus gave orders to set fire to the gates of the temple. Shortly after this, the sacred temple itself was burnt down, even against his consent.

Two of the legions completed their banks on the eighth day of the month of Loios.[1] Titus ordered that battering rams should be brought, and set against the western edifice of the inner temple. Before these were brought, the strongest of the other war machines had battered the wall for six days without stopping but made no impression on it. The massive and strongly connected stones were superior to those war machines, and to the other battering rams also.

Other Romans undermined the foundations of the northern gate, and with great struggle removed the outer stones, yet the gate was still held up by the inner stones and stood strong. The sappers gave up all attempts by battering rams and prybars and brought their siege towers to the colonnades. The Judeans could not stop them from doing this, but after they had climbed up, attacked them and fought with them. Some of them they knocked back down or threw them back down head first. Others they fought and killed. They killed many more who tried to climb up ladders, killing them with their swords before they raised their shields to protect themselves. Some of the ladders they knocked over from above when they were full of armed men.

A great slaughter was made by the Judeans at that time. Even those who carried the ensigns fought hard for them, viewing it as a terrible thing and a great shame if they permitted them to be stolen away. After some time, the Judeans captured the siege towers and destroyed those who had gone up the ladders. The rest were so intimidated by what had happened to those who were killed, that they retreated, although none of the Romans died without having done his service before his death. Of the rebels, those who had fought bravely in the former battles did the same now, among them Eleazar, the nephew of Simon the tyrant. When Titus saw that his attempts to spare a foreign temple turned to the detriment of his soldiers, and they were being killed, he gave orders to set the gates on fire.

During this time, Ananus from Emmaus deserted to him, along with most of Simon's most vicious guards, and Archelaus, the son of Magadatus. They still hoped to be forgiven because they left the Judeans at a time when they were still being victorious. Titus objected to these men being forgiven, viewing it as a cunning trick of theirs, and as he had been informed of their other barbarities towards the Judeans, he wanted to have them killed immediately. He told them that they were only driven to desertion because of the terrible distress they were in, and did not come in good faith. That they did not deserve to be saved, as they had set their own city on fire, and now they were just running from the fire. However, the amnesty he had promised deserters overcame his resentment, and he dismissed them accordingly, however, he did not give them the same privileges that he had given others.

The soldiers had already put fire against the gates, and the silver that was coating them quickly carried the flames to the wood that was within. Therefore, it spread very quickly and caught engulfed the colonnades. When the Judeans saw this fire all around them, their spirits sunk together with their bodies, and they were so astonished, that not one of them tried to either defend himself or quench the fire, but they stood like mute spectators. However, they did not so grieve at the loss of what was now burning, to learn something for the next time because the sacred temple had itself been on fire already, they vented their hatred against the Romans. This fire continued during that day and the next, as the soldiers were not able to burn all the colonnades that were around it at one time, but only in sections.

The next day, Titus ordered part of his army to quench the fire and to make a road for the legions to march more easily, while he gathered the commanders together. Those assembled included the six principal people: Tiberius Alexander, the commander of the whole army, Sextus Cerealis, the commander of the fifth legion, Larcius Lepidus, the commander of the tenth legion, Titus Frigius, the commander of the fifteenth legion, Eternius, the leader of the two legions that came from Alexandria, and Marcus Antonius Julianus, procurator of Judea. With these came all the rest of the procurators and tribunes.

Titus asked them to advise him on what to do about the sacred temple. Some of these thought it would be best to follow the rules of war because the Judeans would never stop rebelling while the temple was standing, as it was where they always assembled. Others of them thought that if the Judeans would leave it, and none of them would store weapons in it, he should spare it. However, if they refused and continued to fight, he should burn it, because then it should not be viewed as a temple but as a citadel. If so, the impiety of burning it would then belong to those that forced this to be done, and not to them.

Titus replied, "Although the Judeans should hide within that temple, and fight us from there, still we should not avenge ourselves on inanimate things, but on the men themselves." He was not under any circumstances in favor of burning down such a vast work as it was, because this would be villainous to the Romans themselves, as it would enhance their government while it continued.

Fronto, Alexander, and Cerealis grew bolder in their declaration and agreed to the opinion of Titus. When this assembly was dismissed, Titus gave orders to the commanders that the rest of their forces should remain still, but that they should send the most courageous to this attack. He commanded that the chosen men that were taken out of the cohorts should make their way through the ruins, and put out the fire.

On this day the Judeans were so tired and so confused that they refrained from any attacks. But on the next day, they gathered their whole force together, and attacked those who guarded the outward court of the temple very aggressively, through the east gate, and this was about the second hour of the day.

These guards fought their attack with great bravery and covered themselves with their shields. They formed up into something like a wall, drawing their squadron close together. Nevertheless, it was clear that they could not last there very long, but would be overwhelmed by the multitude of those that sortied out against them, and by the heat of their hatred. However, Caesar saw this from the tower of Antonia, that this squadron was likely to give way, and he sent some cavalry to support them. Then the Judeans found themselves unable to sustain their assault, and when those in the forefront were killed, most of the rest retreated. However, as the Romans were retreating, the Judeans turned upon them and attacked them. As those Romans turned back toward them, they retreated again, until about the fifth hour of the day, when they were overwhelmed and locked themselves in the inner court of the temple.

Titus returned to the tower of Antonia and decided to storm the temple the next day, early in the morning, with his whole army, and to lay siege to the temple. As for that temple, God had certainly long ago doomed it to fire. Now that fatal day had come, according to the revolution of ages.

It was the tenth day of the month Loios, on which it had formerly been burned by the king of Babylon, although these flames were started by the Judeans themselves, and were caused by them. When Titus left, the rebels waited a little while, and then attacked the Romans again, when those who guarded the temple fought with those who were putting out the fire that was burning the inner court of the temple. These Romans caused the Judeans to retreat and followed as far as the temple itself. At this time, one of the soldiers,

without waiting for any orders, and without any
concern or dread upon him at so great an undertaking,
and being inspired by a certain divine fury, grabbed
some of the burning debris and being lifted up by
another soldier, through the fire through a golden
window. On the inside, there was a passage to the rooms
that were around the temple, on the north side of it. As
the flames spread upward, the Judeans made a great
noise, as this event warranted, and ran to prevent it.
They no longer fought to save their lives, nor tried
anything to stop their force, since the temple was
burning, and they had been stationed around it to
prevent this from happening.

Someone came running to Titus, and told him about
the fire, as he was resting in his tent after the last battle.
He got up quickly and ran as he was to the temple to
order the burning to be stopped. Behind him trailed all
his commanders, and after them followed several legions
in great surprise. There was a great clamor and tumult,
as was natural in the disorderly motion of such a great
army.

Caesar called to the soldiers that were fighting with a
loud voice, and also gave them a signal with his right
hand, ordering them to put out the fire. But they did not
hear what he said, though he shouted loudly because
their ears were filled with the greater noise around

them. They also didn't see the signal he made with his hand, as some of them were still distracted with fighting, and others with passion.

As the legions came running in, neither any persuasions nor any threats could restrain their violence, but each one's own passion was his commander. As they crowded into the temple, many of them were trampled by one another, while a great number fell among the ruins of the colonnades, which were still hot and smoking and were destroyed in the same terrible way as those who they had conquered. Once they had approached the temple, they acted as if they did not hear Caesar, and they encouraged those who were before them to set it on fire. As for the rebels, they were in too great distress already to put out the fire. Their dead lay everywhere in and around the temple. The majority of the people were weak and without arms, and had their throats cut wherever they were captured. Around the altar lay dead bodies heaped one upon another. A great quantity of their blood ran down the steps going up to the altar, as the dead bodies that were killed above it fell down there.

As Caesar was not able to hold back the enthusiastic fury of his soldiers, and the fire grew more and more, he went into the sacred place in the temple with his commanders, and saw it and what was in it. He found it to be far superior to what its foreign relatives contained, and not inferior to what we ourselves have bragged regarding it and believed about it. As the flames had not yet reached its interior, and were still consuming the rooms that were surrounding the temple, and Titus thought that the temple might still be saved, he rushed in and tried to persuade the soldiers to put out the fire. He ordered Liberalius, a centurion, and one of the spearmen who were near him to beat the soldiers who were disobeying with their staves and to force them.

However, their passion was stronger than the respect they had for Caesar, and the dread they had of he who forbade them. Their hatred of the Jews was also too strong, with a vehement desire to fight them. Moreover, the hope of plunder induced many to go on, believing that all the places within were full of money, and seeing that all around it was made of gold. One of those who went into the place forbidden by Caesar, ran in so quickly past the soldiers posted there to restrain them, and threw fire onto the hinges of the gate, in the dark. The flame burst out from within the sacred temple itself immediately. Then the commanders retreated, and Caesar with them, and then nobody forbade those who intended to set fire to it. And so the temple was burnt down, without Caesar's sanction.

Anyone would justly lament the destruction a work like this, since it was the most beautiful of all the works that we have seen or heard of, both for its curious structure and its size, and also for the vast wealth invested in it, as well as for the glorious reputation it had for its sacredness. Yet one might comfort himself with this thought, that it was the fate decreed to it, which was inevitable, both for living creatures and also for works and places. However, one cannot but marvel at the accuracy of this period relating to it, for the same month and day were now observed, as I said before when the sacred temple was burned by the Babylonians. The number of years that passed from its first foundation, which was laid by King Solomon, until its destruction, which happened in the second year of the reign of Vespasian, add up to be one thousand one hundred and thirty, plus seven months and fifteen days. From the second building of it, which was done by Haggai, in the second year of King Cyrus, until its destruction under Vespasian, there were six hundred and thirty-nine years and forty-five days.

Peshitta 5th Maccabees: Chapter 4 Notes

1 Lôios (Λώιος) was the tenth month of the Macedoninan calendar, which followed the previously mentioned month of Panamos.

Peshitta 5th Maccabees: Chapter 5

The great distress the Judeans were in after the burning of the sacred temple. Concerning a false prophet, and the signs that preceded this destruction.

While the sacred temple was on fire, everything was plundered that could be carried. Ten thousand of those who were caught were killed. There was no compassion shown to any age or any pity for reason, but children and old men, and profane people along with priests were all killed in the same manner. This conflict encompassed all sorts of men and brought them to destruction, as well as those who begged for their lives, as those who defended themselves by fighting.

The flame was also carried a long way, and made an echo, together with the groans of those that were killed. Because this hill was high, and the works at the temple were very great, one would have thought the whole city had been on fire. One cannot imagine anything either greater or more terrible than this noise. There was at once a shout of the Roman legions, who were marching all together, and a sad clamor of the rebellious, who were now surrounded with fire and sword. The people that were left above were beaten back by the enemy, and in great horror, made sad moans at the trouble they were in.

The multitude that were in the city joined in this outcry with those who were on the hill. Besides this, many of those who were worn away by famine, and their mouths almost closed, when they saw the fire of the sacred temple, they exerted their last strength and broke out into groans and cries again. Pera returned the echo, as well as the mountains around the city, and augmented the force of the entire noise.

Yet the misery itself was more terrible than this noise, for one would have thought that the hill itself, on which the temple stood, was seething hot, as every part of it was on fire. The blood was larger in quantity than the fire, and those who were killed more in number than those who killed them, for the ground was no longer visible because of the dead bodies that lay on it. The soldiers climbed over heaps of those bodies, as they chased those who fled from them.

It happened that when the bulk of the thieves were driven out of the inner court of the temple by the Romans, they had a great struggle getting to the outer court, and from there into the city, as the remainder of the populace was fleeing into the colonnade of that outer court. As for the priests, some of them picked up the spikes around the sacred temple with their lead bases and shot them at the Romans instead of arrows.

Then, as they gained nothing by this, and fire burst in upon them, they retreated to the wall that was eight cubits wide and remained there. Two of these eminent men were among them, who might have saved themselves by surrendering to the Romans or have carried on courageously, and taken their fortune with the others. Instead, they jumped into the fire and were burned with the sacred temple. Their names were Meirus, the son of Belgas, and Joseph, the son of Daleus.

The Romans decided that it was pointless to spare what was around the sacred temple, and so burned all those places, along with the remains of the colonnades and the gates, except two: the one on the east side, and the one on the south. Both of which, however, they burnt afterward. They also burned down the treasury chambers, in which was an immense quantity of money, and an immense number of garments and other precious goods stored there. To summarize, there was all the wealth of the Judeans piled up together, where the rich people had built rooms there to contain furniture.

The soldiers also came to rest in the colonnades that were in the outer court of the temple but found there the women and children, and a great mixed multitude of the people who had fled, in total about six thousand. Before Caesar had decided anything about these people, or given the commanders any orders regarding them, the soldiers were in such a rage, that they set that colon-nade on fire. Because of this, it happened that some of these died by jumping down, and some were burned in the colonnades. None of them escaped with their lives.

A false prophet was the cause of these people's destruction, who had made a public proclamation in the city that very day, that God commanded them to get into the temple, and that there they would receive miracu-lous signs of their deliverance. There were at the time, many false prophets hired by the tyrants to impose their will on the people, who told them, that they should wait for deliverance by God.

This was to keep them from deserting, and that they might be bolstered above fear and care by such hopes. A man who is struggling easily complies with such prom-ises. When such a seducer makes him believe that he will be saved from the misery that oppresses him, then he becomes like the patient who is full of hope for his survival.

Therefore the miserable people were convinced by these deceivers, and such as told lies as if coming from God himself. They did not pay attention to or give credit to the signs that were so evident, and so obviously predicted their future desolation, but, like men infatu-ated, without either eyes to see or minds to consider, they did not regard the denunciations that God made to them.

Thus there was a star resembling a sword, which hung over the city, a comet that continued for a whole year. Also before the Judean rebellion, and before those troubles that preceded the war, when the people had come in great crowds to the feast of unleavened bread, on the eighth day of the month Xandikos,[1] and at the ninth hour of the night, such a great light shone around the altar and the sacred temple, that it appeared to be bright as daytime. This lasted for half an hour. This light seemed to be a good sign to the foolish but was so interpreted by the sacred scribes as to portend those events that followed immediately upon it. At the same festival also, a heifer, as she was led by the high priest to be sacrificed, birthed a calf in the middle of the temple.

Moreover, the eastern gate of the inner court of the temple, which was made of brass, and incredibly heavy and was shut with difficulty by twenty men. It was set on a base made of iron and had bolts fastened very deep into the door frame, which was made of one massive stone. It was seen to open by itself around the sixth hour of the night. Those who kept watch in the temple ran to the captain of the temple, and told him of it, who then went there, and not without great difficulty was able to shut the gate again. This also appeared to the commoners to be a very happy event, as if God had done this to open the gate of happiness for them. But the men of learning understood that the security of their sacred temple was dissolved of its own accord and that the gate had opened for the advantage of their enemies. These publicly declared that the signal foreshadowed the desolation that was coming upon them.

Besides these, a few days after that feast, on the twenty-first day of the month of Artemisios,[2] a certain prodigious and incredible phenomenon appeared. I suppose the story of it would seem like a fable if it were not told by those who saw it, and the events that followed it were so substantial in nature as to deserve such a signal. Before the sunset, chariots, and legions of soldiers in their armor were seen running around among the clouds surrounding the city. Moreover, at that feast which we call Pentecost, as the priests were going by night into the inner court of the temple, as their custom was, to perform their sacred ministrations, they said that at first they felt a quaking and heard a great noise, and after that they heard the sound as of a great crowd were saying, "Let us leave here."

What is still more terrible, is that there was one Jesus, the son of Ananus, a plebeian and a farmer, who, four years before the war began, and at a time when the city was peaceful and prosperous, came to that feast where it is our custom for everyone to make tabernacles to God in the temple, and began suddenly to scream out, "A voice from the east, a voice from the west, a voice from the four winds, a voice against Jerusalem and the sacred temple, a voice against the bridegrooms and the brides, and a voice against this whole people!"

He cried this day and night, in all the streets of the city. However, some of the most eminent among the populace had great indignation at this dire cry of his and captured the man, and whipped him a great many severe stripes. Nevertheless, he didn't either say anything for himself, or anything against those who punished him, but still went on with the same words that he had yelled before. Our rulers, supposing the case was proven, that this was a sort of divine fury in the man, brought him to the Roman procurator, where he was whipped until his bones were exposed, yet he did not beg for himself, nor shed any tears, but turning his voice to the most lamentable tone possible, at every stroke of the whip his answer was, "Woe, woe to Jerusalem!"

When Albinus who was then our procurator asked him who he was, where he came from, and why he said such things, he did not try to reply to what he had asked but still did not stop his mournful song. Albinus took him to be a madman and dismissed him. During all the time that passed before the war began, this man did not go near any of the citizens, nor was seen by them, but he uttered these lamentable words every day as if it were his premeditated vow, "Woe, woe to Jerusalem!"

He did not curse any of those who beat him every day, nor blessings to those who gave him food. This was his reply to all men, and indeed none other than a melancholy prediction of what was to come. This cry of his was the the loudest at the festivals, but he continued this song for seven years and five months, without growing hoarse or getting tired of it, until the very time that he saw his prediction fulfilled by our siege. When it ended he was going around upon the wall and cried out as loud as possible, "Woe, woe to the city again, and to the people, and to the sacred temple!" Also, he added at the end, "Woe, woe to myself also!" Then a stone flew out of one of the catapults and hit him, killing him immediately. As he was stating the very same prediction his spirit left him.

If anyone considers these things, he will find that God takes care of mankind, and in all ways possible to warn our people about what is to be done for their preservation. Men die by the misery which they madly and voluntarily bring upon themselves. The Judeans, by demolishing the tower of Antonia, had made their temple four-square, while at the same time they had it written in their sacred oracles, "Their city would be captured, as well as their sacred temple when their temple should become four-square."

But now, what did the most elevated of them do during this war? They found an ambiguous oracle that was found in their sacred writings, how, "about that time, one from their country should become governor of the habitable earth." The Judeans took this prediction to belong to themselves in particular, and many of the wise men were therefore deceived in their determination. Now this oracle certainly denoted the government of Vespasian, who was appointed emperor in Judea. However, men can't avoid fate, although they see it beforehand. These men interpreted some of these signals according to their own pleasure, and some of them they completely hated, until their madness was demonstrated, both by the capture of their city and their own destruction.

Peshitta 5th Maccabees: Chapter 5 Notes

1 Xandikos (Ξανδικός) was the sixth month on the Macedonian calendar, and happened roughly equivalent to March on the Gregorian calendar.

2 Artemisios (Ἀρτεμίσιος) was the seventh month on the Macedonian calendar, which was approximately at the same time as April in the Gregorian calendar.

Peshitta 5th Maccabees: Chapter 6

How the Romans carried their ensigns into the temple and made joyful acclamations to Titus. The speech that Titus made to the Judeans when they made supplication for mercy. What reply they made, and how that replied moved Titus' indignation against them.

After the rebels fled into the city, and after the burning of the sacred temple itself, and all the buildings around it, the Romans brought their ensigns to the temple and set up against its eastern gate. There they offered sacrifices to them, and they declared Titus victorious with the greatest celebration of joy. All the soldiers had such vast quantities of the plunder that they had pillaged, that in Syria a shekel[1] weight of gold was sold for half of its former value.

As for those priests that still remained up on the wall of the sacred temple, there was a boy who, out of his thirst, wanted some of the Roman guards to give him their right hands as a security for his life, and confessed he was very thirsty. These guards pitied his age, and the distress he was in, and so gave him their right hands. He came down and drank some water, and filled a jug that he had with him when he came to them, and then sneaked away and ran back to his friends. None of those guards could catch him, but still, they insulted him for his deceitfulness. He replied, "I have not broken the agreement. The safety I asked for was not so I could stay with you, but only in regards to my climbing down safely, and collecting some water. I did both these things, and so see myself as having been faithful to my agreement."

After this, those who the child had fooled admired his cunning because of his age. On the fifth day afterward, the priests that were dying from starvation came down. When they were brought to Titus by the guards, they begged for their lives. He answered that the time of pardon was over for them, and it was only because of the sacred temple they could justly hope to be saved, but it was destroyed. It was agreed by their office that the priests should die with the temple itself to which they belonged, so he ordered them to be put to death.

As for the tyrants themselves, and those who were with them, when they found they were surrounded on every side, and, as it were, walled in without any route of escaping, they wanted to negotiate with Titus face to face. Therefore, because of his kind nature, and his desire to preserve the city from destruction, along with the advice of his friends, who now thought the robbers had come to their senses, he went to the western side of the outer court of the temple. There were gates on that side above the portico and a bridge that connected the upper city to the temple. This bridge stood between the tyrants and Caesar and divided them, while the multitude stood on each side. Those of the Judean nation around Simon and John, with great hopes of pardon. The Romans around Caesar, in great anticipation of how Titus would receive their supplication.

Titus ordered his soldiers to restrain their rage, and to stay their arrows, and appointed an interpreter between them, which was a sign that he was the conqueror, and began the conversation first, saying, "I hope you men are now satisfied with the misery of your country. You have not had any reasonable concepts of either of our great powers or of your own great weakness. Like madmen acting in a violent and inconsiderate manner, engaged in actions that have brought your people, your city, and your sacred temple to destruction. You have been men who have never stopped rebelling since Pompey first conquered you, and have, since that time, made open war with the Romans. Have you depended on your multitude, while a very small division of the Roman soldiers have been strong enough for you? Have you relied on the honesty of your confederates? Which nations are there, out of the boundaries of our empire who would choose to assist the Judeans against the Romans?"

"Are your bodies stronger than ours? No, you know that the strong Germans themselves are our servants.

Have you stronger walls than we have? Please, what greater obstacle is there than the wall of the ocean which surrounds the Britons? Yet cannot defend against the arms of the Romans. Do you exceed us in courage of spirit, and in the wisdom of your commanders? No, indeed, you must know that even the Carthaginians were conquered by us. It can therefore be nothing but the kindness of us Romans which has excited you against us, who, in the first place, have given you this land to possess. Secondly, we have set over you kings from your own nation, and, third, have preserved the laws of your forefathers for you, and have permitted you to live by them, either by yourselves or among others, as it should please you."

"What is the greatest favor we have given you? Permission to collect the tribute which is paid to God with the other sacrifices that are dedicated to him. We have not called those who collected these donations to account, nor prohibited them. Eventually, you became richer than we ourselves, even when you were our enemies. Did you prepare for war against us using our own money? No, after all, when you enjoyed all these advantages, you turned your surplus against those who gave it to you, and, like merciless serpents, have spit out your poison against those who treated you kindly."

"I suppose that you might have hated the laziness of Nero, and, like limbs of the body that are broken or dislocated, you did then remained quiet, waiting for some other time, though still with a malicious intent. Now you have shown your hatred to be greater than ever, and have extended your desires as far as your impudent and immense hopes would enable you to do."

"When my father came into this country, it was not with a plan to punish you for what you had done under Cestius but to admonish you. If he had come to overthrow your nation, he would have moved directly to your fountain-head, and immediately destroyed this city. Instead, he went and burned down Galilee and the neighboring regions, and therefore gave you time to repent. You mistook this act of humanitarianism for an act of weakness and fed your impudence on our mildness. When Nero had left the world, you acted like wicked wretches, encouraged yourselves to act against us through civil dissent, and abused that time when both I and my father had traveled to Egypt to prepare for this war."

"You were not ashamed to raise rebellion against us when we were made emperors, and this after you had experienced how mild we had been when we were simply generals in the army. When the government was given to us, and all other people remained peaceful, and foreign nations sent ambassadors and congratulated our ascension to the government, then you Judeans showed yourselves to be our enemies. You sent ambassadors of your nation that are beyond Euphrates to help you raise a rebellion. You built new walls around your city, and seditions arose. One tyrant struggled against another, and a civil war broke out among you, and as such you became a cursed people."

"Then I came to this city, as I had been unwillingly sent by my father, and received sad injunctions from him. When I heard that the people were disposed to peace, I rejoiced. I advised you to stop all this before I began this war. I offered to spare you, even when you had fought against me for a long time. I gave my right hand as security to the deserters. I observed what I had promised faithfully. When they fled to me, I had compassion on many of those who I had taken captive. I tortured those who were eager for war, to stop them. I brought my war machines against your walls reluctantly. I always prohibited my soldiers, when they were intent upon your slaughter, from their severity against you."

"After every victory, I offered you peace, as though I had been defeated. When I approached your temple, I again abandoned the laws of war and advised you to save your own sanctuary and preserve your sacred temple. I allowed you a peaceful exit and security for your safety. If you had wanted it, I offered you safe passage to fight in another place. Yet you have still rejected every one of my proposals, and have set fire to your sacred temple with your own hands!"

"Now you vile wretches, you want to negotiate with me face to face? What could have caused you to save such a sacred temple as this was, which is now destroyed? What hope of survival can you now have after the destruction of your temple? You are still standing there in your armor right now, and cannot bring yourselves to even pretend to be suppliants, even in this, your final hours! You miserable creatures! What do you depend on? Are your people not dead? Is your sacred temple not gone? Is your city not in my power? Are your own lives not in my hands? Do you still think it's glorious to die?"

"I will not imitate your madness. If you throw down your arms and surrender to me, I grant you your lives. I will act like a mild master of a family. What cannot be healed shall be punished, and the rest I will save for my own reasons."

They replied to Titus offer, stating that they could not accept it because they had sworn never to. They wanted a path to leave through the wall that had been erected around them, with their wives and children. They would go into the desert, and leave the city to him. At this Titus had great indignation, that when they were already captured men, they should pretend to make their own terms with him, as if they had been conquerors.

He ordered this proclamation to be made to them: That they could no longer come over to him as deserters, nor hope for any further safety. From then on, he would spare nobody, but fight them with his whole army. That they must save themselves as best they could, as that from then onward he'd treat them according to the laws of war. He gave orders to the soldiers both to burn and to plunder the city. They did nothing that day, but on the next day, they set fire to the archives, to Acra, to the council-house, and to the place called Ophlas. At that time the fire spread as far as the palace of Queen Helena, which was in the middle of Acra. The streets were also burnt down, as were those houses that were full of the dead bodies of those killed by famine.

On that day, the sons and brothers of King Izates,[2] together with many others of the eminent men, got together and begged Caesar to give them his right hand for their security. Although he was very angry at all who were now remaining, did he not put aside his former moderation and listened to these men? At that time, he took them all in custody and chained the king's sons and relatives. He took them with him to Rome to make them hostages for their country's submission to the Romans.

Peshitta 5th Maccabees: Chapter 6 Notes

1 Syriac: tql (ܬܩܠ). Translation: shekel

2 Syriac: zûṭûś (ܙܘܛܘܣ). Translation: Izates

Izatês II (Ἰζάτης) was the king of the kingdom of Adiabene in northern modern Syria between 31 and 54 AD. His family had converted to Judaism and many of his brothers and children were in Jerusalem when the Romans conquered it. At the time, Adiabene was likewise occupied by the Parthian empire, and, likely, the two countries were covertly cooperating in an attempt to free them both.

Peshitta 5th Maccabees: Chapter 7

What happened to the rebels after they had caused a great deal of problems, and suffered many misfortunes. And also how Caesar captured the upper city.

The rebels rushed into the royal palace, into which many had moved their belongings because it was so strong, and drove the Romans away from it. They also killed all the people that had crowded into it, who were about eight thousand four hundred in total and plundered them of what they had. They captured two of the Romans alive. One was a cavalryman, and the other an infantryman. Then they cut the throat of the infantryman and immediately had him dragged through the whole city as if revenging themselves on all the Romans through this one act.

The cavalryman had suggested to them that keeping him alive might help them save themselves. Therefore he was brought before Simon, but when he had nothing to say when he was there, he was given to Ardalas, one of the commanders, to be punished. He tied his hands behind him, put a blindfold over his eyes, and then brought him out in front of the Romans, intending to cut off his head. But the man prevented his execution, by running away to the Romans while the Jewish executioner was drawing his sword. When he had escaped the enemy, Titus could not think of putting him to death.

However, he considered him unworthy of being a Roman soldier, as he had been captured alive by the enemy. He took away his weapons and threw him out of the legion. For one with a sense of shame, it was a penalty worse than death itself.

On the next day, the Romans drove the robbers out of the lower city and set all on fire as far as Siloam. These soldiers were glad to see the city destroyed, but they found nothing to plunder, because the rebels had carried off all their effects, and had retreated to the upper city. They did not yet regret the troubles they had caused, but were insolent, as if they had done well. When they saw the city on fire, they appeared cheerful and put on joyful pretenses, in expectation, as they said, of the end of their misery. However, as the people were now dead, the sacred temple was burned down, and the city was on fire, there was little left for the enemy to do.

Nevertheless, Josephus did not grow tired, even in this utmost extreme, in begging them to spare what was left of the city. He spoke to them about their barbarity and impiety and gave them his advice for their survival. He received nothing back other than being laughed at by them. They could not think of surrendering, because of the oath they had taken. Yet they were not strong enough to fight the Romans any longer, as they were surrounded on all sides, and already a type of prisoner.

Yet, were they so accustomed to killing people, that they could not restrain their right hands from it? They dispersed themselves into the city, and laid in ambush among its ruins, to catch those who attempted to desert to the Romans. Many such deserters were caught by them, and all were killed. These were too weak because of being starving, to escape from them, so their dead bodies were thrown to the dogs.

Now every other sort of death was thought more tolerable than the famine, in that, though the Judeans despaired now of mercy, they would attack the Romans, and would themselves, even of their own accord, fall among the murderous rebels also. There was no place in the city without dead bodies in it. It was entirely covered with those who were killed either by the famine or the rebellion. Everywhere was full of the dead bodies of those who had died, either by that rebellion or by that famine.

The last hope which supported the tyrants, and that band of robbers who were with them, was in the caves and caverns underground. If they could just escape, they did not expect to be searched for. They considered that after the whole city would be destroyed, and the Romans had left, they might come out again, and escape. This was no better than a dream of theirs, for they were not able to lie hidden either from God or from the

Romans. However, they depended on these underground subterfuges and set more places on fire themselves than the Romans did.

Those who fled out of their burning houses fled into the caverns. They killed without mercy and pillaged them also. If they discovered food belonging to anyone, they grabbed it and swallowed it, together with their blood also. They turned to fight one another during their plunder. and I cannot but think that had their destruction not prevented it, their barbarity would have made them eat even the dead bodies themselves.

Peshitta 5th Maccabees: Chapter 8

How Caesar raised siege mounds around the upper city and when they were completed, gave orders that the war machines should be brought. He then conquered the whole city.

When Caesar saw that the upper city was so steep that it could not possibly be taken without raising mounds against it, he delegated several parts of that work among his army. This was on the twentieth day of the month of Loios. The conveyance of materials was a difficult task since all the trees, as I have already stated, which were around the city within the distance of a hundred stadions, had their branches cut off already, to make the previous mounds.

The works that belonged to the four legions were erected on the west side of the city, near the royal palace. The whole body of the auxiliary troops, with the rest of the multitude that were with them, erected their banks at the portico, from which they reached the bridge, and the tower of Simon, which he had built as a citadel for himself against John, when they were at war with one another.

It was at this time that the commanders of the Edomites got together in private, and discussed surrender to the Romans. They sent five men to Titus and asked him to give them his right hand for their security. So Titus thinking that the tyrants would surrender if the Edomites, upon whom a great part of the war depended, withdrew from them, after some reluctance and delay, agreed with them, gave them security for their lives, and sent the five men back.

As these Edomites were preparing to march out, Simon found out and immediately killed the five men who had gone to Titus and imprisoned their commanders, of whom the most eminent was Jacob, the son of Sosas. The multitude of the Edomites did not know what to do now that their commanders were taken from them. He had them watched and secured the walls by a more numerous garrison, yet that garrison could not stop those who were deserting. Although a great number of them were killed, there were still more deserters.

They were all received by the Romans because Titus himself grew negligent as to his former orders for killing them, because the very soldiers grew tired of killing them, and because they hoped to get some money by sparing them. They left only the populace and sold the rest of the multitude with their wives and children, and every one of them at a very low price because so many were sold, and the buyers were few. Although Titus had made a proclamation beforehand, that no deserter should come alone by himself, so they might bring out their families with them, still he received these also. However, he set over them those who were to distinguish some from others, to see if any of them deserved to be punished. Indeed the number of those that were sold was immense, but from the populace, over forty thousand were saved, whom Caesar let go wherever any of them pleased.

At this time one of the priests, Jesus the son of Thebuthus, after having his security given by the oath of Caesar, that he should be saved, upon condition that he should bring to him some of the precious things that had been deposited in the temple, came down, and delivered to him from the wall of the sacred temple two candlesticks, like those that lay in the sacred temple, with tables, and cisterns, and vials, all made of solid gold, and very heavy. He also delivered to him the veils and the garments, with the precious stones, and a great number of other precious vessels that belonged to their sacred worship. The treasurer of the temple, whose name was Phineas, was seized, and showed Titus the coats and girdles of the priests, with a great quantity of purple and scarlet, which were there deposited for the uses of the veil, as also a great deal of cinnamon and cassia, with a large quantity of other sweet spices, which used to be mixed together and offered as incense to God every day. A great many other treasures were also delivered to him, with many sacred ornaments of the temple. For the things delivered to Titus, this man obtained from him the same pardon that he had allowed to those who deserted of their own free will.

The siege mounds were finished on the seventh day of the month of Gorpiaios,[1] after eighteen days, then the Romans brought their war machines against the wall. Some of the rebels, despairing of saving the city, withdrew from the wall to the citadel. Others went down into the subterranean vaults, although a great many of them still defended against those who brought the battering rams. Nevertheless, the Romans overcame them by their number and their strength.

The main thing was that they continued their work cheerfully, while the Judeans were quite depressed, and became weak. As soon as part of the wall was battered down, and some of the towers yielded to the impression of the battering rams, the rebels fled away, and such a terror fell upon the tyrants, which was much greater than the occasion required. Before the enemy got over the breach they were quite stunned, and immediately ran away. Now one might see these men, who had previously been so insolent and arrogant in their wicked practices fall down trembling, in that it would pity one's heart to observe the change that was made in those vile persons.

Therefore, they ran with great violence at the Roman wall that surrounded them, in order to force away those who guarded it and to break through it, and get away. When they saw that those who had formerly been faithful to them had gone away, as indeed they fled wherever the great panic they were in caused them to flee, as also when those who came running before the rest told them that the western wall was entirely knocked down, while others said the Romans had gotten in, and others that they were near, and searching for them. These were the only dictates of their fear, which imposed upon their sight. They fell on their face, and greatly lamented their own mad conduct. Their nerves were so terribly loosed, that they could not run away.

Here one may chiefly reflect on the power of God exercised upon these wicked wretches, and on the good fortune of the Romans. These tyrants did now wholly deprive themselves of the security they had in their own power, and came down from those very towers of their own accord, whereas they could have never been taken by force, nor indeed by any other way than by famine. And so the Romans when they had taken such great pains about weaker walls, received through good fortune what they could never have gotten by their war machines for three of these towers were too strong for all mechanical engines whatsoever, concerning which we have described above.

So they left these towers of themselves, or rather they were ejected out of them by God himself and fled immediately to the valley that was under Siloam, where they again recovered themselves out of the dread they were in for a while, and ran violently against that part of the Roman wall which lay on that side. As their courage was too depressed to make their attacks with sufficient force, and their power was now broken with fear and affliction, they were repulsed by the guards, and dispersing themselves at distances from each other, went down into the subterranean caverns.

The Romans became masters of the walls, they placed their ensigns upon the towers, and made joyful celebrations for the victory they had gained, as having found the end of this war much easier than its beginning. When they had seized the last wall without any bloodshed, they could hardly believe it, but seeing nobody to oppose them, they stood in doubt what such unusual quiet could mean. When they went in numbers, into the lanes of the city with their swords drawn, they killed those who they captured outside and set fire to the houses the Judeans fled into, burned everyone in them, and destroyed a great many of the others. When they had come to the houses to plunder them, they found in them entire families of dead men, and the upper rooms full of dead corpses, that is, those who died in the famine. They stood in horror at this sight and went out without touching anything.

Although they had sorrow for those who died in that way, they had no sorrow for those who were still alive. They killed everyone they met, blocked the lanes with their dead bodies, and made the whole city run with blood, to such a degree that the fire of many of the houses was quenched by these men's blood. Although the killers quit in the evening, the fires spread greatly during the night, and as all was burning, began the eighth day of the month Gorpieus upon Jerusalem, a city that had been witness to so much misery during this siege, that, had it always enjoyed as much happiness from its first foundation, it would certainly have been the envy of the world. It did not on any other account deserve so much of these sore misfortunes, as by producing such a generation of men that were the cause of this its destruction.

Peshitta 5th Maccabees: Chapter 8 Notes

1 Gorpiaios (Γορπιαῖος) was the eleventh month of the Macedonian calendar, roughly equivalent to August in the Gregorian calendar.

Peshitta 5ᵗʰ Maccabees: Chapter 9

The injunctions Caesar gave when he came into the city. The number of the captives and of those who perished in the siege. Also concerning those who had escaped into the subterranean caverns, among whom were the tyrants Simon and John themselves.

When Titus had entered the upper city, he admired some places of strength in it and in particular the strong towers which the tyrants in their madness had run from. When he saw their solid altitude, the largeness of their stones, and the exactness of their joints, and also how great was their depth, and how extensive their height, he said, "We have certainly had the gods as our assistants in this war, and it was none other than the gods who threw the Judeans out of these fortifications. What could the hands of men or any war machines do to knock down these towers?"

At the time, he had many conversations with his friends. He also let free those who had been imprisoned by the tyrants and were left in the prisons. To conclude, when he entirely demolished the rest of the city and pulled down its walls, he left these towers as a monument of his good fortune, which had defeated his auxiliaries, and enabled him to capture what could not otherwise have been captured by him.

Since his soldiers were already quite tired of killing men and yet there appeared to be a vast multitude still remaining alive, Caesar gave orders that they should kill those who opposed them but should capture the rest alive. Together with those who they had orders to kill, they killed the old and the infirm, but for those who were in their flourishing age, and who might be useful to them, they drove them together into the temple and locked them up within the walls of the court of the women.

Caesar set over them one of his freed-men, and also Fronto, one of his own friends, who was to determine everyone's fate, according to his merits. Fronto executed all those who had been rebels and robbers, who were accused one by another. But of the young men, he chose out the tallest and most handsome and reserved them for the triumph march. As for the rest of the multitude that were above seventeen years old, he put them into chains and sent them to the Egyptian mines. Titus also sent a great number to the provinces, as a present to them, so they might be destroyed in their coliseums, by the sword and by the wild animals. Those that were under seventeen years of age were sold as slaves.

During the days when Fronto was judging these men, eleven thousand more starved to death. Some of them did not eat any food because of the hatred of their guards. Others would not eat any when it was given to them. The multitude was so very great, that they were short of enough grain to keep them alive.

The number of those who were taken captive during this whole war adds up to ninety-seven thousand. The number of those who perished during the whole siege was eleven hundred thousand, the majority of whom were of the same nation as the citizens of Jerusalem, but not from the city itself. They had come from all across the country for the feast of unleavened bread and were suddenly trapped by an army, which, in the beginning, seemed so appropriate, but later there came a pestilential destruction upon them, and soon afterward such a famine which destroyed them more quickly.

That this city could contain so many people in it, is manifest by the number of them which was captured by Cestius, who wanted to inform Nero of the power of the city, who would otherwise have been disposed to contemn the nation, asked the high priests if it was possible to count their whole multitude.

These high priests, when that feast of the Passover happened, killed their sacrifices, from the ninth hour until the eleventh, made sure that each group was not less than ten for each sacrifice, as it is not lawful for them to feast by themselves, and many of us were twenty in a group. They found the number of sacrifices was two hundred and fifty-six thousand and five hundred, which, upon the allowance of no more than ten who feast together, amounts to two million seven hundred thousand and two hundred people that were pure and holy. As to those who have leprosy, gonorrhea, or women that have their menstruation periods, or are otherwise unclean, it is not lawful for them to partake of the sacrifice, nor for any foreigners either to come here to worship.

This vast multitude was collected from remote places, but the entire nation was now trapped by fate like in a prison, and the Roman army surrounded the city when it was crowded with inhabitants. Accordingly, the multitude of those that perished there exceeded all the destructions that either men or God ever brought upon the world. To speak only of what was publicly known, the Romans killed some of them, some they took as captives, and others they searched for underground, and when they found where they were, they broke up the ground and killed all they found.

There were also found dead more than two thousand other people, some by their own hands, and some by one another, but mostly killed by the famine. Then the disgusting stench of the dead bodies was most offensive to those who found them, so much so that some immediately ran away, while others were so greedy of gain, that they would go in among the dead bodies that lay on heaps, and climb upon them. A great deal of treasure was found in these caverns, and the hope of profit made every way of getting it to seem lawful.

Many of those who had been imprisoned by the tyrants were now brought out. They did not end their barbarous cruelty until the very last, yet God avenged himself on them both, in a manner agreeable to justice.

As for John, he starved together with his brothers in these caverns and begged that the Romans would give him their right hand for his security, which he had often proudly rejected before. Simon struggled hard with the distress he was in until he was forced to surrender himself, as we shall discuss later, so he was reserved for the triumph march, and then to be killed. John condemned to perpetual imprisonment, and now the Romans set fire to the outer parts of the city and burned them down, and entirely demolished its walls.

Peshitta 5th Maccabees: Chapter 10

While the city of Jerusalem had been captured five times before, this was the second time it was destroyed. A brief account of its history.

Jerusalem had been captured in the second year of the reign of Vespasian, on the eighth day of the month Gorpiaios. It had been captured five times before, though this was the second time it was destroyed. Shishak, the king of Egypt, and after him Antiochus, and after him Pompey, and after them Sosius and Herod, captured the city but preserved it. Before all these, the king of Babylon conquered it, and destroyed it one thousand four hundred and sixty-eight years and six months after it was built. But he who first built it was a potent man among the Canaanites, and is in our own tongue called Melchizedek, the Righteous King, for this he was. On this account he was the first priest of God there, built the first temple there, and called the city Jerusalem, which was formerly called Salem.

However, David, the king of the Judahites, ejected the Canaanites and settled his own people there. It was demolished entirely by the Babylonians, four hundred and seventy-seven years and six months after him. From King David, who was the first of the Judahites who reigned there, to this destruction under Titus, were one thousand one hundred and seventy-nine years.

However, from its first building, until this last destruction, were two thousand one hundred and seventy-seven years. Yet neither its great antiquity, nor its vast riches, nor the diffusion of its nation over all the habitable earth, nor the greatness of the veneration paid to it on a religious account, has been enough to save it from being destroyed. And so the siege of Jerusalem ended.

Lady Shamoni[1] and the Maccabean Martyrs (6th Maccabees)

Who can retell it; the history of the worthy ones of the house of Judas the hammer,[2] describing their intense zeal? They who, for the sake of the orit[3] and for the sake of the commandments entered into competition and struggles; real trials of strength. They were strong men of war; truly powerful. They destroyed armies, as Paul told us. There was no end to their war against bold rulers.

Day in and day out, they found themselves in arms and armor, battling constantly throughout the year. One chased a thousand in power received from the Lord, and two caused ten thousand to flee, through divine aid, which was granted these sturdy ones. They knocked down idols and broke the power of the inscriptions in small idols. They set fire to idols' shrines, and pulled down idols' temples; habitation of satans,[4] as their father, the chief priest had commanded.

They were sons of Mattathias,[5] these upright ones, and because of this cause, they allowed their minds to experience all afflictions. May their prayer be a fortification for believers. Now therefore, we will touch on numerous deeds of amazing people who died for the sake of the truth, endured torment and all punishments because of their hope, received the iron-comb tortures and excruciating executions, and then ascended to the light.

They endured being killed and deaths in various ways; with breaking of legs and amputating of joints; with pulling of teeth, and flaying of scalps; with breaking of bones and dislocating of joints; and nailings and verbal abuse; and white hot sword quenchings, and tongs tearing off flesh; with the sharp points and turning of screws; and sulfur-filled caldrons emitting dense fumes; glowing hot razors cutting tongues and heated iron stakes burning furiously.

They endured all this from he who worshiped the idol, the cursed troglodyte[6] Antiochus, the rabid dog, so that what prevailed over the sufferings of the body was a powerful way of thinking. Their reason governed the pleasures of this transitory world, and their imagination was focused on the world to come. Through this, they won all their struggles, these amazing people. Eleazar, I declare myself, the revered elder, and Shamoni, the faithful martyr, completely hopeful for her seven sons, youths who are handsome, and fair in deeds:

On their account, I, the wretched unworthy one, gave my attention to this description, and on their account I made this short homily, and for their eulogy, I bear on my shoulders this torrid sackcloth. That their *abundant prayers may continually be of help to me, and from the table of their banquet they may give me one crust. That I may complete my mind virtuously, bearing this account.*

They were offspring of Abraham and from that stock. A blessing they have sprouted, these seven wonderful branches. For this reason, that they overcame the devices of the evil master ruler,[7] may their prayer always be a protective wall for us.

When Seleucus, the ruler, passed away from the kingdom, he designated his son to succeed him as ruler, Antiochus, who was full of malevolence.

He dismissed Onias, the priest, from the high priesthood, and installed Jason instead, a mistake, because he offered a bribe of three thousand talents.

He set him in authority over the people and gave him the rulership.

This man altered the Judean way of life and repudiated the law of Moses, profaned observance of the Sabbath undermined observance of the commandments, and annulled circumcision.

During his reign, Antiochus came to Jerusalem and pillaged it.

He entered the temple, and took away all its treasures; the deposits and trust funds of the orphans and the widows.

Within three days he removed eighty thousand; forty thousand of these he forced into slavery in other countries, and forty thousand of these he killed around the city.

The remnant who survived, he amassed in one place and pressured them to abandon the commandments of the orit, desert their customs, and assimilate to the foreigners'[8] customs: that they should taste of the sacrifices to idols; and for food they should eat pork and every other unclean thing, or else they would be tortured to death.

Then the tyrant sat on the high platform of judgment, and he had one after another of the Judeans brought before him.

First of all, they brought before him a distinguished elder whose name they announced as Eleazar the Priest, and he was the instructor of these seven young men and honored by all the people of Israel

The unjust judge began the proceedings, and said to him, "From now on, renounce the Lord[9] and his orit, and eat the sacrifices, and meat of the abominable swine, so that I do not incinerate you in the caldron of the oven.

The fire is prepared, and will destroy your life quickly with great malice."

Eleazar, the noble priest, answered out loud and said courageously to him, to Antiochus the serpent, "I am not convinced by your words, oh mistaken king. I do not fear your threats since it is neither possible, nor useful, nor righteous, nor fair that I refuse the holy food, the sacrifice of the Lord, and instead, I should eat polluted and impure sacrifices and corrupt flesh. How is it possible for me to renounce him, the god of the living,[10] El Shaddai,[11] creator of the land as well as the skies, and love engraved and senseless idols, the works of the hands? Constructions of dirt and porous clay molded with water. Plated in silver and gold, and that was not even pure, constructed from wood and precious stones. Diverse creations, the works of a human being, subject to desires, are sold at inflated prices. Works that have eyes and do not see, appearing blind; that have mouths and no breath in them, laying there like the dead. How could I repudiate the orit of Moses, the greatest prophet, and become a laughing stock after I have grown old and advanced in years and leave behind an evil name for the ages coming after me? What is the point of living any longer? You wretch, bring your torturers to me. Bring your hardened scourges so strong! Heat your caldron, stoke your roasting fire, and put me to death, indeed, and I am exchanged for the chosen people."

Then the transgressor, the horrid one, commanded them to strip the clothes off that had modestly covered the martyr and to leave him naked, that venerable elder. When they had stripped him bare, they immediately tied up his hands and feet, and they pulled him around and began to hit him with all kinds of scourges, with cruel rods and leather whips and all sorts of torturous devices until his flesh was torn to bits and his blood ran down on the ground.

Then they brought the holy one near the burning fire, and each of them held in his hand a skewer that they heated in the fire, before skewering him shamelessly.

When he fell to the ground, they kicked him, those spawn of demons. He endured it calmly, the righteous, distinguished elder because he looked for the future kingdom.

When servants of the tyrant saw the elder, that he did not flinch, they doubled the punishment to his intense affliction and also poured sewage into his nostrils, the idol-worshippers and brought instruments devised with cunning, and they scourged him and dragged him into the burning fire, now glowing.

When his bones caught fire and he knew it the moment of his end and freedom in the skies, he called out loud, this chief of the venerable ones, "See, God, and do not forget the work of your hands, and spare your people. Do not at all turn your face from us, and may your truth dawn for the ransom of your servants, and may it not be hidden. Know now, I yielded my body to every tribulation on their behalf. For their redemption, may my blood be purified, as though it were a drink offering."

When he had said all this, he died, his face shining, as he had inherited a life that has no end. After the breath of the holy martyr had left, the evil tyrant burned with desire or rage and was carried away in his anger. He saw that his suppression of the Hebrews was accomplishing nothing.

He commanded that they bring others from the gathered people, and they dragged in, first of all, the martyr Shamoni, that noble mind, while her sons surrounded her like a garland, two with another five. When the wicked one saw that with one banner of victory, they were coming before him, he was carried away with passion.

He admired their beauty and their innocence, which was undefiled, and he hid his ill will inside his mind, the murderer, and he brightened his face, the audacious one, so excited, and he began to seduce them through confusing words: "I have heard of your tradition, that it is from a blessed source and, indeed, you have acquired reason and discerning intellect. I desire of you, blessed youths, that you immediately eat pork and polluted sacrifices. Don't let yourselves become like that unfortunate elder who caused his own life to end in harsh tortures and lacerated flesh. If instead you don't resist and obey my words from now on, I will give each of you power over a separate matter and you will also be clothed in garments, from inside-out wrappings that I have chosen, and you will be of those who eat at my table morning and evening. If instead, you rashly remain in your errant inclination, I will bring upon you affliction and punishment. I will tear off your limbs with the wheel and with a sharpened sword. I will fry you on the iron frying pan and in brass caldrons, and I will burn you with the strong fire that is kindled. I will scatter your dust in the wind that carries off error, and I will make you into mud, treading you underfoot."

Then the lawless evil one commanded his worthless servants to bring and arrange in front of them all kinds of torments so that he could frighten and terrify them, the just ones. They brought ropes and secure shackles with leather straps, and wedges together with hands of iron and combs that tear the flesh, and the revolving wheel full of cutting teeth, and skewers and cunningly invented irons for separating limb from limb, and frying pans and caldrons glowing with fire, full of torments.

Then the evil tyrant said to them, to the heroes, "Abandon your ancient customs, and renounce the law of your ancestors, and judgment decrees, and be joined with me and I will make you important in my kingdom. Or else I will immediately crush your backbones with these "tools," and you will be hurled into these sizzling caldrons and disappear from this world."

Then the martyrs replied wisely, in one voice, as if from one mind and from one mouth they said the same words, "Bring your tortures, evil and sinful tyrant. Bring your bitter blows, perverse foolish moron, and we will endure them for our law, without fear, and we will not renounce the law of Moses, not a single word. We will not bow down to senseless idols that have no speech. If our exemplar overcame your tortures and your mighty sword and despised your scourgings and was not brought low by your threatening, he who was old in years and already an elder having grown weak. How then will we, who are young men and mighty warriors, be subdued before your contemptible tortures, liar, fool! Enough, you have said enough, shut your deceitful mouth. We are choosing to die for the creator of everything. It is delightful to us that we should burn up in the flaming fire rather than we should obey your word, you perverted destroyer! We know that if you cut us in pieces without cause, our Lord will receive us into royal dignity and set a crown on us. Our minds will be taken up into the houses of light, and we will enjoy the company of Abraham the faithful, and be welcomed. While you, in agony, in the burning light of Gehenna[12] will be made a filthy, disgusting thing. Your mind will be with demons in the darkness, enduring pains because the Lord granted you reason and intelligence and understanding, but you became an animal that does not speak."

When the tyrant king heard these words, he raged and burned in his passion and anger, and was covered in envy. He commanded his servants who were standing before him at the time to bring the eldest, that worthy one.

His mother, the elder, came near to be with him, her mind firmly set, and heartened and strengthened him, and said to him this, "Look to me, my son. This is the time to administer to you an oath by El Shaddai so that you are well-strengthened and unflinching in this contest, and as you went first in the birth of nature, and were first-born among them in the world that is now ending, so you shall be first-born among them in the world we are awaiting."

After she had spoken to him, they dragged him before the judge. But first, they tore his tunic and stripped him, and tied his feet and his hands with leather straps. The sons of satan scourged him with whips that were very cruel and had no pity. When they saw that their torture was something that had gained them nothing, they set him on a wheel and stretched him out upon it, a method of torture.

When his joints were dislocated by that affliction, and his bones were broken by the pain-inflicting wheel, he reviled the judge and said, "You little king, impure one, the enemy of the king of the skies, and a poisonous snake in regards to reason, intellect, and understanding. You aren't tormenting me like this because I killed anyone, nor because I have contrived wickedly against God, or not even that I have been evil, but because I am brave on behalf of the law of my ancestors."

The impure ones replied to him, "Confess without delay and you will not be destroyed."

He answered them, "Your wheel has no power at all. See, you just bring on all your tortures. As you cut off my limbs with my joints and cook me in the frying pan, you'll see how our nation is invincible."

When they heard these words they lit a fierce fire under him, and they forced him onto a wheel, made cruel by artifice. The wheel was soaked in his blood pouring out, and from the dripping of his blood, the fire was quenched. When the flesh had melted onto the spokes of this machine, and his bones had been torn apart, he did not cry for help.

The strong and heroic young man, a faithful son of Abraham. However, be was not destroyed, but transmuted. He steadfastly endured tortures without number, and said, "Become like me, my brothers, and from this, my command forever, let your love never leave and do not renounce your brothers for the sake of a life that is transitory. Work nobly and gloriously with me today, and pray diligently to him, who is the righteous judge, so he may bring punishment upon this rapacious wolf."

When he had said these words he surrendered his worthy life and inherited the kingdom, the light, and the bridal chamber.

Blessed are you, saintly Gaddi.[13] *They worked their wickedness so that you would apostatize, and you said to them, "This is my plan. That if you cut off my feet and my hands and if you tear in pieces my limbs, all of them, with my ligaments, and if you then cut off my joints with my arteries, and if you flay my skin and destroy my skeleton, and if you add double the abuse to my tortures, and if you add the harshest of all agonies to my torments, I am bearing them without disturbance in a heart that rejoices. I am not obeying you, and I am not changing the things I do, and I am not repudiating the law of my ancestors and my customs, and I am not renouncing my God, El Shaddai."*

After that, the mind of the youth was translated to the kingdom, and then she approached the second, their mother, the distinguished elder. She strengthened him and fortified him and heartened him by means of words: "Be strengthened, my son, and do not be unmindful of the love of the brothers, and consider your brother, how he endured suffering for an hour and inherited life without ceasing and without end, and you now suffer and remain for an hour in perseverance, and you will inherit the life that does not end in the new world."

After his mother, the worthy one had encouraged him, they seized him and hung him, the evildoers, that very hour, and right away they brought out and gloved their unclean hands in iron gauntlets that had sharpened fingernails. They asked him whether he was willing to eat from the sacrifice, and when the idol-worshippers heard the courageous words of the martyr, they put the long fingernails behind his head and they stripped the skin of his head along with that of his shining face. In this way they killed him, the leopard-like animals!

That same one, then, had honorably endured torture, and cried out, "How sweet is the form of this death, that it is for the sake of the law and faithfulness of our fathers."

He rebuked the judge and said, "You one full of wickedness, you are more cruel than all other tyrants, and full of evil. I know that you are more tormented than I am because you see that we have confounded the glory and pride that covers you. We have destroyed all your strategies, leaving you shamed. As for me, sufferings are sweet to me, in victory. As for you, your punishment is being held for you in Tartarus[14] eternal darkness without end, and devouring fire."

After the martyr, marvelous in exploits, had said these words, he ended his life with great merits. Know that he is now delighting in the pleasures of Eden.

Blessed is your commemoration, oh holy martyr Maccabee! How you endured the struggle and followed in the steps of your brother. Your feet did wander from the path that your brother had marked and when your ribs were separated by the cruel wheel, and your fingers were cut off by a sharp razor, and your glowing face had been torn with iron fingernails, you did not call out because of that torture! Instead, your courageous words vexed the madman. You made sounds that confounded the tyrant Antiochus, and the army of demons left because of your victories. Through your intercessions on behalf of Israel, they were redeemed, and your prayers ascended to the skies.

After this martyr had died and inherited peace, Shamoni went up to the third among these victorious ones, like one who carries lambs to the butcher, and she embraced and kissed him with affection and longing.

"Look, my son, pay attention and do not forget the love of your brothers, and may their remembrance never be erased from your mind. See how they endured and inherited lives of rest, and call to mind our ancestors Abraham and Isaac, the deceased ones. Do not forget the law of Moses, which was written on tablets. Never let the killing of your brothers be erased from before your eyes. Instead, imitate them and endure for an hour, for if you die, you will live."

Then, after she had encouraged him, the ravenous wolves seized him and they gave him things to eat that had been offered to impure idols, and sacrifices, and many had begged him to eat so he would live.

He replied to them, "You evil and headstrong lawless ones, didn't a single father beget us all, you confused ones? This mother, didn't she give birth to my brothers, beloved and honored? Didn't she, the one and the same, carry me in her womb for nine months, and from two breasts we suckled milk many times? It is obvious all of us are the same as one of us, read lessons, portions of scripture, and yet you say, 'Deny your brothers, tortured one after the other!' Am I less than my brothers, you empty ones? It is good for me to die with my brothers in terrifying tortures, and not obey you, you elevated demons!"

When the troglodyte had heard this from the mouth of the youth, and when he repeated these words, he was inflamed with passion and rage, and brought instruments for separating the joints and bones and all parts of the body, and they began. First, his hands and feet were cut off and separated. His fingers, forearms, and elbows they severed, and they crushed the shins of his legs together with the joints of his knees. When they found out they could not contend with him, they put him on the wheel, that separator of limbs.

When his flesh had been torn open, he called out, "You wicked one of tyrants! We endure all tortures for the sake of our law. You, however, because of your wickedness, commit evil beyond all acts of evil. Because of your slaughter of those who have not sinned, know that which falls on you will be bitter tortures which have no beginning and no end."

And when he had said these words he died, the one valued among gold coins of great worth, and he inherited a life that is forever and ever.

I am astonished by your endurance, purified by sprinkling one, and my meditation about your story does not cease, day or night. How you were tried with every kind of trial because this was your portion, and these were the lots of your portion so that from the top of the wheel there should be a towering castle of splendor for you, and also on that torture instrument, you spread covers on the couches of the peace of your mind. Although your cartilages were ripped apart and your ribs, you called out, "I will not renounce my brothers Instead, I am dying with them for the sake of my laws, and for the sake of my customs I yield my earthly concerns to this slaughter. From the top of the wheel, I will receive from the Lord assurances of the perdition of this little price and viper."

You are a worthy one, as you put the foundation on this rock of hardest stone through your faith, and your hope in Jesus the unshakable. Through your prayers, all the sons of the tribe of Israel were saved, and the altar on the Jebusite section was at peace. May your prayers be given for our sins' remission.

After the martyr had ended his life, victorious in all, Shamoni approached the fourth, valiant among the zealous ones, and encouraged him and strengthened him in words and in aids, though her heart burned and her eyes tiered, "Be strengthened, my son, and have no fear at all of the sufferings they bring on you, these accursed ones and deceivers. Do not renounce the law of your ancestors, and the established accounts, the writings of Moses, all-fulfilled, the first-born of all the prophets. Consider, my son, your brothers, how they died as martyrs, because of the tortures at the will of that tyrant who they held in contempt. Even though at this hour you endure the pain of confessors, you will soon inherit life that does not end, with Abraham, Isaac, and Jacob, the righteous men you will take delight in those blissful houses."

After she had encouraged him, they came up to him, those minor princes, and whipped him and said, "Obey us and do not be insane like your brothers, who have destroyed their minds. Eat flesh of sacrifices, and every-thing you hate, and you will be honored by the king with honor and gifts."

He answered them, "No, you destroyers! If you want to frighten me, ignite the hot fire, and bring your insane tortures, and see how I will overcome them with great strength. Nothing, not the deaths of my brothers, who are full of heavenly joys, and not the eternal destruction of the tyrant, with the adversaries, and not the lives of the true ones, who are beyond time, will make it so that he did not destroy my brothers and my loving relatives. Now send far and wide, you tyrant more evil than all other tyrants, for new torturers, that through them you may learn for all time that I am a full brother of those who have shamed you, you one full of conniving! I will make their goal of a rational mind my own."

Then when he heard these words to such a degree of defiance, he thirsted for slaughter, the wicked and impure Antiochus. He immediately commanded the soldiers that the son's tongue be cut out first. Then the son said, "Even if the instrument of my voice weakens him. The exalted God will hear even the silent. See, my tongue has been stuck out for you, let them cut it out from inside the mouth right now! I am pleased when I give the majority of every limb to destruction, on behalf of God, without pause or begrudging. The tongue of my mind, you tyrant, you cannot cut out! The just ones of God will be avenged on you quickly, as this tongue praises the Lord by night and by day. So, cut away, you evil and wicked, and cursed one!"

Then they inflicted on him tortures and scourges of bitter perversity, and he finished his life and inherited pleasure.

Lady Shamoni and the Maccabean Martyrs

Your commemoration is sweet, oh martyr Hebron, watchers[15] and humans will consider you with amazement. Even demons, rulers of the abode of the powers, will be thrown down by you, and those who bow down to idols will be conquered by your amazing story, and then they will be raised up worthy by your ways. Your name will be remembered in prayer every day by the synagogue. When the transgressor wished to deal shamefully with your pure body, and he made the iron skewers for your scourging white hot, and your holy hands were tied with leather straps, and to loosen the vertebrae of your back in instruments fashioned so cunningly, and from every side thrust into your sides with broad spears, you said, "How sweet is death to those that have been tortured in shameful ways, and that they may die on behalf of the law, without turning to apostasy!" In your prayers, may believers find help.

Then, after this noble witness had completely finished the course, the honorable elder Lady, approached her fifth son and persuaded him, with passion and weeping, and asked of him, and spoke to him in the Hebrew language, "Be persuaded by me, my son, and do not be the foreigner among your brothers. Do not dread the tortures that they construct for you, the deceivers, and remember your brothers and your teacher, the chosen elder. Do not renounce the law of Moses, the ancient prophet. Do not falter in this contest and do not succumb. If you finish your life during these harsh afflictions inflicted on you, our Lord will transport you to the kingdom of the sky, and place a crown on your head that shines until the last day."

When he heard these words spoken from his mother's mouth, he jumped up and stood in the middle before the foolish judge and said, "I will not wait, you miserable tyrant, to start these afflictions on behalf of undefiled Truth. Of my own will, I have done this, and not from harsh coercion. When you afflict me with many tortures, you acquire many sins, and you will be judged guilty, you insane one. Punishment will come upon you from the highest king. What of evil have we done, you hater of the human race? What is the reason you kill us in this hate-filled scheme? Just because we are worshiping the Creator, and meditating in his law by day and by night? This deserves honor and not insult, but because you do the business of Satan, you begin immediately, without delay."

When Antiochus heard these things, he, being inspired by his demons, immediately commanded the evil-minded servants who stood before him, and right away they tied him quickly, and brought him to a block. They tied him to it, and the lawless ones pushed cruel irons into his knees. They bent his back onto wedges with the piece of wood under him, and like a scorpion, he had been bent backward from his neck and they had dislocated his bones, all of them, both the vertebrae of his back and his limbs.

When they afflicted the breath of the holy one like this, he said, "Your torments have given us many benefits: to prove, oh tyrant, that in the power of cruel pains, they have given us prove our power to endure, which is for the law."

With a small sound, his life passed away.

Great and amazing is the story of your contest, oh martyr Hebzon, and all people, even if they agreed together, could not search out a copy of your marvelous conflicts, nor by searching thoroughly could they settle by agreement your splendid struggle. Not even if they should urge the feet of their mind in the path of your tortures, still they will not gain strength to envision the goal of your victory, but if they constrained themselves for a night and a day, then they will be strengthened, and they will go up to the arena of your battle, and there will leap for joy. They will envision you when you were bound on the board, and they will hold fast and will exult in the day of your killing, that upon their faces, that they were delivered from an evil power.

They will learn how you endured torment, so they will not be deprived.

Treasures of your wisdom should not be spoiled by the lustful ones who desired to afflict you, and that they would break the vertebrae of your back was what they sought, and that they would tear out your eyes. They delighted in piercing your palms and your insteps with nails from a vessel of boiling water and in the coming Day of Judgment from God, their sinners will be pierced and upon the wooden planks of suffering in Sheol,[16] they will be justly nailed, against thorn-bushes of fire they will stumble.

When Shamoni saw her son, who received merit, she held back her affections, and she returned to the sixth captive, and she encouraged him and helped him courageously. She embraced him and kissed him from love, and convinced him, saying "The beloved of my mind, blessed son, I implore you, do not be deprived of that inheritance which your brothers have inherited, and do not stay remain without a part, and do not stand alone without the portion that has already reached your brother in the glorious dwellings of the kingdom with Abraham, and Isaac, and Jacob, the ancestors."

After she had encouraged him, the distinguished elder, his mother, then at this point they approached him, regarded him intently, the servants of contention and tied him and whipped him and pressured him so that he would eat of the sacrifice, and the unjust judge and head of heathendom said to him, "Be persuaded by my words and do not be mad with that madness. That maddened your brothers, so that I destroy you, with them, in wrath."

The mighty strong youth replied, "I am younger in years than my brothers, still youthful, nevertheless I am as old as they in the rational mind and in sound thought. Each alike, in some measure, we were born, and each alike we grew up completely into full stature and for their sake, it is just that we die in equality. If, therefore, it has been revealed as of old to you, oh fraudulent one. That if I do not eat, you will torture me with cruelty. Then, forced to submit my body to you, corrupter of youth, seek for yourself the opportunity, and cause your anger to rest upon me in this hour."

When he heard these words from the mouth of the youth, he who was the worst of accursed ones, he commanded the insolent servants who stood before him should bring this youth in particular before him and put him on the top of the wheel. They quickly rushed to carry out the command of the sinner, and they stretched him brutally on the cruel wheel, those impure ones, and the vertebrae of his back were dislocated, crippling all his limbs. Then some of them brought fire and placed it under him, and some of them pierced him with long iron skewers they had heated. They pierced and skewered him, those merciless ones, and his bowels and arteries and intestines they burned.

Then, when he was being tortured with these horrors, he said, "Hurray for the glorious conflict that is full of good things! Which attach to it the conflict for the sake of the truth you had trampled."

For, then, to all these pains all these brothers were summoned, and it ended with none of them defeated as they were unconquerable, whatever the defilement of one full of evils.

"I love being put to death with these five brothers, of destructive demon, and inventor of all torture. See, now, your fire has cooled and your irons are not burning me, because the divine lance-bearers surround us."

When he heard these words from the mouth of the martyr, that inhabitation of demons commanded that they take him down from the wheel. His limbs had been mangled and he had him put in the caldron and boiled him. Those compassionless ones ended his life, which had been full of all good things.

Sweet is your commemoration and great is your victory, oh martyr Baukos, who withstood so many

*cruelties and tortures from Antiochus, that sinner, trans-
gressor-in-chief, Epiphanes, who contrived his network
of lies for capturing you, and with knives smeared with
a deadly ointment he sought to kill you.*

*You conquered him and put to an end his strategies
with a miracle of God, and you were never abased, nor
did you bow down before that person striking, more
lawless than all, and the inhabitation of demons of
Gehenna. You endured the bitterest of deaths, as well as
all peril and you did not agree with the counsel of the
evil one, nor renounce the law of Moses the prophet,
which he brought down on tablets, from the Mount.
You did not yield to the enticements of the one void of
understanding, like a Greek boy. Instead, you emulated
your brothers and the theologian Eleazar, the dignified
elder, your own instructor. Beautifully you confessed
your Lord before that whole crowd which Antiochus,
the Antichrist, gathered against you.*

*As the writer of their story, Josephus recorded it.
Because of this, El Shaddai made you a deathless one and
gave you power over his treasure houses and over
everything shared in common and made you one who
sees mysteries, a contemplative, and put upon your head
a diadem of light, a crown. Your prayer will preserve all
of them, children of one inheritance.*

When Shamoni saw her son, that he had honorably finished the course of his life, she approached her seventh son and said, "Be strengthened, my son, and let nothing weaken your grasp on his crown. Consider your older brother, how much he enticed him, but he reviled him and scorned his ostentation and his haughtiness. Now you also, oh beloved of my mind, be like him and do not be afraid of the evil one, and his menace, and do not be flattered by his beguiling enticements."

When they saw her encouraging him more than her other sons, they took hold of him, tied him up, and brought him before the king. The tyrant, as if with compassion, grieved for him, for this young one who was shorter than the rest in height. When he saw that he was bound with bonds, he summoned him, and from the very spot where he stood with him, he brought him up close to him.

"My son, do not be insane with the madness of your brothers," he said to him, "For each one of them, by means of his madness has destroyed himself, and presents and honors and favors I give to him, and whoever does not obey me, but stiffens his neck, every terrible affliction I bring upon him. I cut up his body with this cruel wheel and inside caldrons, these bubbling ones, I burn him!"

The unjust judge summoned the son's mother next and had her brought, so that when she saw that she was now about to be deprived of all of them, perhaps she would lead him so that he would be obedient to the words of the most sinful one, and would listen to his counsel.

She said to him in the Hebrew tongue, "Beware, my son, of this impure one, and of his impurity. Be very brave for an hour in the law of Moses, and do not renounce it, or on the day of judgment each of your brothers has received his crown, and you lose the crown of light that has been kept for you."

Then he answered and said to the king and all of them, his people, "Release me from my shackles!"

They obeyed his voice and quickly released him because they supposed that he agreed with their counsel. Instead, he ran to one of the cauldrons that was near him and reviled the king, and spoke to him and said, "You wicked king, woe to you! Your treachery is greater than all wickedness! You who does not stand in awe of God your maker from whom you received every good thing, and their rulership he has given you, who would kill his servants, the athletes, when they have not sinned against you. Because of this, the judgment of God is being kept just for you. Fire more intense than this is ready to burn you, and torture you for eternity without end, they are being kept just for you. Against whom have you behaved arrogantly, and against whom have you raised your voice? Against him who gave you mind and mouth, and who created your speech, and from mute elements that have no speech he made you. For because of this, it has come near, the day of your recompense has arrived. I, then, I too am prepared that I may die, and I say to you, 'I have not denied my brothers who were killed by you.' I have cried out to God that he will requite you according to your work, and in this world and the world beyond he will torture you."

When the saint had said these words, and praying that all would come upon that tyrant in fulfillment, he hurled himself into their basin that was a frying pan, and finished his life and died in great pain.

They sang praise on the day of your commemoration, oh martyr Jonadab, you who rebuked Antiochus like Elijah did Ahab when he gathered a company of soldiers and seditious roughnecks and a mob and grew great against you, and with all their torturings and all their blows, made war against you and you overcame him and frustrated his scheme, and he earned condemnation, and by means of your endurance, marvelous to report, he has been found exceedingly guilty, and because of this, the tale of your victories became famous in all the world.

The report of your strength in the contest is known among all nations. How you entered the refiner's fire of temptations and came forth as gold, and your body was fried in the frying pan, and your flesh was melted, and your heart did not convulse from the pains, nor did your mind break down. Each of the good ones who had died had prepared to offer himself up for they, from that blessed band of the House of Maccabee, had each been crowned. The seven-member group was made perfect through martyrdom when they finished and the group received unfading crowns of light in the kingdom.

Shamoni, the faithful martyr, remained behind, alone, and also was bereft of the seven beloved sons. Moreso she was separated from the nest of seven chicks, and, like a dove that moans by day and by night, she moaned, like a swallow that twitters, she was twittering. It seemed good to her for her sons to be crowned together with her, and she was yearning to be settled in a home with those in the kingdom. When she was about to be possessed by the impure ones, for slaughter, and their hands would have damaged her pure body against her will, except that she at once leaped into that burning fire, and there in that bitter fire she was crowned, and with the righteous, her mind was comforted.

How good and honorable is your commemoration, Oh martyr Shamoni! Your name gives pleasure on the roof of the palate and is better than honey to the mouth. For when the accursed one rebuked your sons with tortures, right in front of you, and through him their souls were taken away to the country of the righteous. Your rational mind and your wisdom did not depart from you, and your enduring courage restored the rational mind of the youths. By the power of your counsel, their childish reasoning was reconstituted, and therefore not one of them complied with the words of the fool. From their eagerly desired slaughter, he gained no advantage. Instead, by their dear deaths the wretched one gained shame, and therefore your amazing story is told over and over again among all nations, and congregations in the four quarters of the world are built in your name. Your name is reckoned among the righteous. You are blessed, oh martyred mother of seven boys! How could you have set at nothing, trampled under foot, passions of all kinds?

When you stood with your seven sons and you observed Eleazar while the lawless one inflicted torment on him? And you said, in the Hebrew language, 'Oh brothers, great is this struggle to which we have been called, for the testimony of our people and the law of our fathers. Take heart, my sons, have no fear, and be heroes. It would be such a shame that this distinguished elder should endure pains for his fear of God, and you, who are young, should turn aside from these tortures and *shrink from death. Keep in mind that we are in this life for the sake of God, and on account of this, it is fitting that we should endure all troubles. Observe our father Abraham, father of all nations, in what manner he bound Isaac tightly, and put him on pieces of wood and put a knife to the throat of him who was the son of the promises. He did not tremble, for the reason that he expected an unending life. Lay hold of the firm faith of these, and if it is that you do not weaken, and you remain strong facing the tortures. You will then inherit life that is for eternity.'*

My brethren, these men of wonder thus rose up like flames in the pure fear of God and they encouraged one another while saying, in their courageousness, "Let us imitate the three young men of the House of Hananiah. Those who were in Assyria, scorning the blazing fire."

One said, "My brothers, Let us not weaken through cowardice."

This other one said, "Let us endure, my brothers, through fortitude."

Another said, "They will call to mind our family, from whence it came."

Then every one of them, while being filled with gladness, said, "Come, let us commend our hearts to the giver of souls. He will raise our bodies for the sake of the law and the precepts."

So come, my brothers, let us be prepared in self-mastery with a rational mind that is above pains, and let us not be tempted with terror, for if we thus taste death on account of our law, Abraham and Isaac, the ancestors will receive us, and also all our ancestors will celebrate us with rejoicing and will make merry with us in the kingdom.

6th Maccabees Notes

1 Syriac: mrtå šmônî (ܫܡܘܢܝ ܡܪܬܐ). Translation: Lady Shamoni

Mrtå (ܡܪܬܐ) is often rendered as a name as the Greeks adopted the word as the name Martha (Μάρθᾱ), which spred across Europe, however, this is the Syriac word for 'Lady.' It was translated as 'Lady' in both Hebrew Maccabees and Arabic Maccabees, both of with drew on Judeo-Aramaic source texts. The word is translated directly here from the Syriac as 'Lady.'

2 Syriac: yhůdå lmkkbå (ܡܟܒܐ ܝܗܘܕܐ). Translation: Judah the mkkba

The nickname mkkba is derived from the Judeo-Aramaic word for 'hammer,' mkkbå (מכבא). This term was transliterated into Greek as 'Judas the called Maccabeus'

(ΙΟΥΔΑϹ ΟΚΑΛΟΥΜΕΝΟϹ ΜΑΚΚΑΒΑΙΟϹ) at the Library of Alexandria, resulting in his more common English name of Judas. In the late-Classical era Hebrew Book of the Hammer (Hebrew Maccabees), Judah's father claims that he is known as the mkbyy (מכבי״) because of his strength, confirming that the term was interpreted as meaning 'hammer' for centuries after the life of Judah. His more common English name of Judas is used in this translation.

3 Syriac: åůrytå (ܐܘܪܝܬܐ). Translation: orit (or torah, laws)

4 Syriac: śtnyn (ܣܛܢܝܢ). Translation: satans (or devils, rivals, adversaries)

The term stnå (ܣܛܢܐ) was used in medieval Syriac the same as the word šaytān (شَيْطَان) Arabic, as a reference to demons and genies that oppose God. In the older Aramaic usage, stnå (ܐܛ߁ܕ) had the same meaning as the Hebrew satan (שָׂטָן), meaning 'contender' or 'adversary.' As the origin of the text is not clear, the term is simply transliterated as 'satans.'

5 Syriac: mty (ܡܬܝ)

Judas' father's name was Mattathias huios Iôannou tou Symeôn (ΜΑΤΤΑΘΙΑϹ ΥΙΟϹ ΙΩΑΝΝΟΥ ΤΟΥ ϹΥΜΕΩΝ) in the Septuagint's 1st Maccabees, which translates as Mattathias son of John the Simeonite, however, the family is generally accepted as having been of the tribe of Levi. The common English version of his name is Mattathias, from the

Greek, however, Mathew would be equally valid as a transliteration.

6 Syriac: bsîlåsq (ܩܣܠܝܣܒ). Translation: basilisk

The Greek term basiliscos (βασιλίσκος) was imported into Aramaic as bsîlåsq (ܐܝܣܒ), which was later imported to Latin as basilisk. The original Greek term means 'lesser prince,' and was used as an insult between the rival kings during the Diadochi Wars. The term took on the same meaning as the Greek t-ôglodytês (τρωγλοδύτης) during the Hellenistic era, which was borrowed back into Greek. The Romans later interpreted the term as a synonym of dracôn (δράκων), resulting in the medieval concept of the basilisk dragon. The earliest reference to the basilisk monster was in Pliny the Elder's Natural History, written in Latin circa 80 AD, however, he described the basilisk as a monstrous cow that killed anyone who saw it. This may have been a historic reference to the Eurasian muskox which, is believed to have gone extinct in Siberia around 550 BC.

As the dating of the text is unclear, there are several possible interpretations. At the time of the event, the term in Greek would have been a disrespectful title to apply to one of the Hellenistic kings. By the beginning of the Christian era, the term would have been the equivalent of 'troglodyte.' Later in the Byzantine era, the translation would have been the equivalent of 'dragon.' As the text is set during the Hellenistic era, but the term is being used as an insult, the translation of 'troglodyte' is used.

7 Syriac: mrå bôlå (ܡܪܐ ܒܠܐ). Translation: master ruler (or lord)

'Strongest of the strong' (𒂊𒈦𒂊𒈦𒈦) was the Neo-Sumerian title for the ruler of multiple lands. This same phrase was interpreted as the 'Ruler of rulers' (𒂊𒈦𒂊𒈦) in Neo-Assyrian, and the 'King of kings' (𒂊𒈦𒂊𒈦) in Neo-Babylonian. The Neo-Assyrian term was adopted into Imperial Aramaic as 'Master ruler' (𐡌𐡓𐡀 𐡍𐡋𐡖𐡉), which is the same term used here in the later Syriac script.

The Neo-Babylonian 'King of kings' was adopted into Old Persian as 'King of kings' (𐎧𐏁𐎠𐎹𐎰𐎡𐎹), the title of the ruler of the Persian emperors. King Seleucus I Nicator adopted the title into Greek as 'King of kings' (βασιλεύς τῶν βασιλέων) when he seized control of what would become the Seleucid Empire. Both terms are used in Judahite literature, with 'King of kings' found in Babylonian, Persian, and Greek-influenced literature, and 'master ruler' in Assyrian and Syriac-influenced literature. This phrase is one of the indicators that the poem was not translated from Greek and likely originated in Aramaic or Samaritan.

8 Syriac: gôyn (ܓܘܝܢ). Translation: nations

The term is a translation of gôyym (גויים), a Hebrew term for foreigners.

9 Syriac: mrå (ܡܪܐ). Translation: master (or lord)

10 Syriac: ålhå ḥyyn (ܚܝܝܢ ܐܠܗܐ). Translation: god living (plural)

11 Syriac: ålšdy (ܐܠܫܕܝ)

The Syriac term is a translation of the Hebrew term El Shaddai (אֵל שַׁדַּי), which had been used in Canaanite since the late bronze age.

12 Syriac: gyhnå (ܓܝܗܢܐ)

Gy hnm (גיא הנם), meaning 'pit of hinns,' is an ancient Semitic term for the land of the hinns that the dead went to. The hinns were a type of firey being that existed in ancient times in Semitic mythology, before being confined to the underworld. This term was translated into Greek as Hades, which was likewise an abode of fire below the world. Gy hnm (גיא הנם) was also used as the generic word for 'grave' in Judahite, generally in regard to a graveyard just outside the walls of Jerusalem that had originally been used by the Amorites.

13 Syriac: gdôå (ܓܕܐ). Translation: lucky

The Christian editor uses the nicknames of the leaders of the later Maccabbean rebellion as the names of the brothers in this poem. In 1st Maccabees, one of Mattathias the son of John's sons was called 'Iôannês o epicaloumenos Gaddi' (ΙѠΑΝΝΗC Ο ΕΠΙΚΑΛΟΥΜΕΝΟC ΓΑΔΔΙ) in the Codex Vaticanus, which translates as 'John nicknamed Gaddi.'

The nickname of gaddi was the Aramaic word for 'lucky' (ܐܕܓ), which is the same word used here, and an indicator that the original text of 1st Maccabees was written in Aramaic. While it is plausible that these Maccabean nicknames were derived from the dead sons of Shamoni, the names of her sons are not otherwise attested, and so it is more likely that the Christian editor of the poem used the nicknames to honor them.

14 Syriac: ṭrṭrûš (ܛܪܛܪܘܣ). Translation: Tartarus

Tartarus (Τάρταρος) was the lowest place in the Greek underworld, a translation used for the Canaanite name šyôl (ܫܝܘܠ), commonly anglicized as Sheol.

15 Syriac: ôyryn (ܥܝܪܝܢ). Translation: watchers (or guardians)

Guardians (or watchers) were a type of sky being in Mesopotamian mythology, descended from the Old Akkadian twin guardians of the sky. The guardians were named Dumuzid and Ningishzida by the Middle Babylonian era, as recorded in the Myth of Adapa, however, appear to have originated earlier as references to the asterisms later known as the constellation Sagittarius and Orion. Sagittarius was known as [deity]Pabilsaĝ (𒀭𒉺𒉈𒊕) during the Sumerian era, however, the etymology was already unclear by this era, theorized to be derived from the proto-Sumerian words for 'archer.' in the Old Babylonian text PBS 10/213, Pabilsaĝ was associated with the god Damu, who by the Middle

Babylonian era had merged with the mythical king Dumuzid to become the guardian Dumuzid.

Assyriologists debate which asterism represented Ningishzida, however, the asterism was reported to spend part of the year in the underworld, meaning, below the horizon as viewed from Iraq. Based on the early references to these two guardians holding up the sky at the edges of the world, it is almost certainly Orion. Orion is at the opposite region of the sky, meaning if one was on the western horizon, the other would be on the eastern horizon. Additionally, Orion does spend part of the year below the horizon as seen from the northern hemisphere. The earliest recorded name for Orion in Mesopotamia was [asterism]Sipazianna (𒆳𒀭𒄑𒈨𒌑𒁯) from the Middle Babylonian era. However, references to the two guardians of the sky go back to Sumerian times. The ancient Greek name Ôariôn (Ὠαρίων) was adopted from the Assyrian name Uruanna (𒀭𒌋𒌋𒀭𒈾), meaning 'light of the sky-stone,' where in 'sky-stone' represented the Neo-Assyrian concept of the vaulted sky made of lapis lazuli.

By the classical era, the guardians had been integrated into Israelite thought, as depicted in the Enochian literature. In the Enochian literature found among the Dead Sea scrolls, some of the ôyryn (𐤏𐤉𐤓𐤉𐤍) had rebelled from the rule of god, and descended to the Earth. This is a story mirrored in Bereshit, where the Aramaic name Nefilim (נְפִילִים) is used instead of irin (עִירִין), the Hebrew translation of ôyryn (𐤏𐤉𐤓𐤉𐤍).

Nefilim (נְפִילִים) is a plural reference to Nplå (ܢܦܠܐ), the Aramaic name for Orion, and likely referred to the Orionids meteor shower that falls in October and early November each year. The meteors fall from the region of Orion's upstretched arm, making it appear the constellation is throwing them down from the sky. Nplå (ܢܦܠܐ) translates as both 'wonderous,' and 'fallen' in Aramaic, which likely gave rise to the mythology of minor gods falling from the sky. In this verse, the context is clearly not the nefilim (נְפִילִים), which are 'fallen watchers,' but ôyryn (ܥܝܪܝܢ), which are watchers still in the sky, and so the translation of 'watcher' is used.

16 Syriac šyôl (ܫܝܘܠ). Translation: Sheol (the underworld)

Sheol was the ancient Canaanite name of the underworld, which was interpreted as Tartarus in the Hellenistic era.

The Story of the Lady[1] and her Seven Sons (7th Maccabees)

My beloved, there was in Antioch, in Syria, a certain woman of the Israelites named Mary,[2] along with her seven sons in the days of the profane and wicked Antiochus.[3] The worshipers of idols told him regarding this woman, "She is a believer," and regarding her sons, "They are believers and holy, for they fear and honor Messiah,[4] the savior of all. They despise and hate the gods, even the statues."

This evil king commanded they should all be arrested and brought before him. Then these brothers were captured, the seven of them and their mother, so that they might release many from sin. As David was sent so he could save Israel from Goliath, God sent this woman like the earlier ones so she might thwart the evil one and save many from his snares.

God is accustomed to thwarting mighty men by the hands of youths, and bringing down the lofty through the hands of women. Through the hands of Gideon and a few people, a multitude of Midianites were destroyed, burnt up, and slaughtered. As for Sisera the evil one who gloried in chariots and cavalry, he was overcome by the hand of Jael,[5] her who God answered. Likewise, Holofernes[6] the commander of the armies of King Nebuchadnezzar of Babylon[7] by the hand of Judith.

Now we come to the story of the Lady[8] (this is Shamoni)[9] and her sons, the victors. Therefore, when she came in and stood in the middle of the battle, and had armed her sons with the armor of the old men who been victorious in battle, the mother gathered her sons and said to them:

"See, my sons, the time of war.

Do not be concerned or afraid, as when you have passed over, degrees of honor will be awarded to you.

Don't tremble before the winter of persecutions, since in the winter the best farmers become known.

Don't be terrified my sons, at this sea with high waves, as from it merchants are spiritually enriched.

Don't be lazy my swift hunters, to leap to meet this lion when he roars against you. Don't be darkened my bright lamps, by the storm of this arrogant one.

Don't be pulled down my strong towers, to ruin your mother.

Don't be persuaded, my flying eagles, by the glittering scales of the snake to go down alive into Sheol.[10]

Don't be afraid, my beautiful doves, of this destroying hawk.

Beware my grape clusters, still full of sweet wine, of the vile fox, or he may make your sweetness bitter.

Don't be afraid, my blameless reapers, the heat of this difficult day.

Don't let be found among you a lie in this glowing furnace. If he flatters you, don't become weak. If he frightens you, don't be terrified. Instead, deal cunningly with him and be cautious with him. If he is angry with you, laugh at him and insult him.

Remember your ancient forefathers and the advantage that they left you in the scriptures. If he shows you unsheathed swords, remember the sharpened knife that was held against the neck of your brother Isaac.

I do not hate you, my sons, that I want you to die, just as your forefather Abraham did not hate his only son when he tied him on the altar to be sacrificed. If I tell you to live in this fleeting moment, I will be proven to hate you and to be robbing you of the eternal life. But like Abraham, who tied up his son not because of hatred but while loving him, and obeyed his God, also I, my sons, love you and your God. I advise you not to remove yourselves from his love. If this profane one shows you scorching fire, remember the three youths, your companions, and how they surrendered their bodies to the fire and did not exchange their worship of God for idols. Don't respect his threats or his flattery but reply to him, 'We will not serve your gods, and will not worship the idols that you have set up.' Even now, my sons, I beg you, be like these, your brothers, and mke me happy.

If he says to you, 'I will throw you to the animals,' remember Daniel who surrendered himself to the lions, so he would not be like those who worshipped statues.

If he says to you, 'I will make you second in my kingdom,' remember Moses your teacher who was made son to Pharaoh's daughter, and he chose to be in distress with God and not to enjoy sin for a short time.

If he promises you riches, remember Joseph who hated the riches of the Egyptian woman.

If he says to you, "Do ye not fear me," remember Elijah the prophet, and how he was not afraid of Ahab the evil king.

Know that you have, my sons, consolation and comfort from your ancient forefathers, and more than anything, the grace of your Lord helps you. I beg you, my beloved,[11] the eldest of all your brothers. Pay me back the loans which I lent you. As I raised you when you were young, support me in my old age. You, my son, contend first in the battle and be victorious, so your brothers can see you and copy you. As you entered this world earlier than them, go ahead of them and enter into the kingdom that lasts forever. What do I have to give you as an inheritance more than this, my son, to love the Lord your god with all your strength and with all your mind? Draw near, therefore, and contend that you may be the firstborn of your brothers in both worlds. If my son, I had engaged wives for you, you would have been the first to enter the bridal chamber, but now you receive a spiritual bridal chamber which will never be destroyed."

She spoke again to all her sons, and said, "I am happy, my sons, when I see you achieving victory. I am happy my sons, when I see that you have passed the drowning sea. I am happy when your grapes will enter the wine press. I am happy when I see you in the fold of the true Lord."

Then they took the holy ones and their mother before the profane king Antiochus, and they stood before him without fear or trembling. When the tyrant saw the beauty of their bodies, and the glory of their faces and the nobleness of their minds, he was astonished and asked them, "Which is the eldest of you all?"

Then the victorious one, the first among his brothers answered, "That is me. What do you want?"

The wicked one answered, "Remember who you are standing before."

The holy one answered and said, "Before a murderous animal."

Antiochus said, "Your life and your death are in my hands, and I have authority over both."

The holy one replied, "You are wrong you poor wretch. You only have authority to destroy the body, but God has authority over the mind."

The king said, "Listen to me and I will enrich you and honor you like those who stand before me."

The victorious one replied, "If only those would obey me, and refuse your riches, which destroy those who possess them!"

The tyrant asked, "Why do you hate your own mind and seek to bring upon yourself horrid torture?"

The illustrious one answered, "I don't hate my own mind but I love it, and I purchase for it with a fleeting life, a life which never ends. But you hate your life, for through these fleeting pleasures you inherit long-lasting pain."

Antiochus said, "Have compassion, poor wretch, on your youth, and don't destroy it."

The athlete said, "Even if you don't destroy it, death comes and destroys it. Therefore, I offer my blood to God, of my own will."

Then the tyrant was irate and commanded him to be beaten with the tendons of a bull until his entire body was lacerated, and they did this to him.

Then the evil one said to him, "See, I have given you the first of the tortures to taste. Obey me or I cut off your limbs."

The holy one said, "If you have worse tortures than these, bring them upon me quickly."

Then the troglodyte[12] commanded that the frying pan be filled with oil, it be brought to a boil, and that he should be fried like a fish while still alive. When the smell of the boiling oil came forth, the holy one went up cheerfully and entered into the middle of the frying pan, and when his body was engulfed in flames, he gave up his mind to the hands of his Lord.

But Shamoni said in celebration, "See one grain of wheat has entered into the treasury of life."

Then she said to her second son, "Go, my son, like the second day on which the firmament[13] was stretched out above the limits,[14] and it separated the waters that are above and the waters which are below. You also, my son, be separated from sinners and join with your brother in good things."

171

Antiochus commanded they should bring the second near him, and he said to him, "Accept my council, my son, as helping you. Look at the face of your brother, and don't say many words."

The blessed one said to him, "Witness the glory of my brother, and don't boast, but quickly send me that I may join him."

Antiochus said, "There is nothing to be seen of the glory of your brother except the body fried in oil."

The holy one replied, "Because your heart is dark with profaneness, you don't see the glory of my brother, but his reproach."

Antiochus stated, "Spare your mind before you enter the frying pan."

The holy one said, "Save your mind before you fall into the Gehenna that is unquenchable."

Antiochus asked, "Don't you fear me, insolent one?"

The victorious one answered, "I don't fear you because you don't fear God."

Antiochus demanded, "Where is your God? Let him come and battle me and save you from my hands."

The illustrious one answered, "He will not save me now, so you may prove your madness and I may prove my faith. He may show his grace, specifically, how he is patient with you, but in the end, he will take righteous vengeance on you, and he will crown me and my brother because of our confession."

Antiochus said, "You only speak words, but I show deeds. Come close and flay the skin off his head like a sheep, and fry him in oil like his brother."

The holy one said, "The athlete deserves to be crowned on his head when he defeats his enemies."

Antiochus said, "As I did to your brother, I am about to do to you, because, like him, you disobeyed me."

The holy one said, "It is right that the neck of the ox should be level with his partner when they work together with the plow. I and my brothers are like oxen that sow in the field of our limbs through your torture. On the day of the resurrection, we will reap from it eternal life."

When he had said these things he gave up his mind to God in the middle of the frying pan.

Shamoni exclaimed, "See two doves have escaped from the wicked hawk and have gone up to their nests in the heights. You also, my third son, quickly go to your brothers who wait for you."

Antiochus said to him, "Come, my son, be with me in this kingdom, and don't be like these wretches, your brothers who destroyed their bodies pointlessly. Obey me immediately and worship my gods."

The holy one answered, "This, your kingdom that you brag about will be dissolved and come to nothing, and likewise the gods you worship. I'm like my brothers, I will surrender my body to torture so I may inherit eternal life with them."

Then Antiochus was angry and commanded to cut off his tongue, his fingers, and his toes. When he had done this to him he gave his mind up joyfully to his Lord.

His mother approached the fourth and said to him, "Know, my son, the form of the fourth who appeared in the furnace to the three youths is engraved on you. You also, my son, quench the wrath of the evil one, and quickly depart to your brothers who wait for you."

Then Antiochus answered, "Worship compassionate gods like me, my son, and don't die like your brothers."

The holy one replied, "I worship God the creator of the skies and earth, and all that is in them. Stones and wood that the carpenters have made, I cannot hear and do not worship. I will not leave the Creator to worship the created. I will not change God, the judge of all, for deaf and blind idols. Sent me quickly to my beloved brothers, as I know they wait for me."

Then the evil one was disappointed in him and commanded to pull out his eyes so he might not see the light of the God of the skies. The holy one said, "It is good you have blinded my eyes so I cannot see your face, evil one!"

When he had insulted him with many stinging words, the tyrant commanded that he should be put to death, like his brothers.

When he brought in the fifth before him, the holy one immediately demanded of him, "What would you ask of me? Shut your mouth while I tell you that if you scalp my head and blind my eyes, and cut off my ears and tongue, I will not obey you, and I will not worship satans.[15] Produce your evil quickly and send me to my brothers, and know they are watching me."

Then, the disciple of Satan commanded that they should cut off his limbs and throw them into the frying pan. Who could see this bitter judgment, half of him alive and half being fried? Yet his mother and his brothers stood adamantly and watched.

He spoke up and said to the wicked one, "Even if you cut off all my limbs, God, as Ezekiel said, is about to gather and raise them up in glory, but your body and your mind he will torture without mercy."

When he had said these things, his mind flew to his brothers and his loved ones.

Shamoni said to her sixth son, "See, my son, Friday,[16] on which man was created is portrayed in you. Don't make the mistake of the first man who wanted to be exalted above his station and lost his glory. Also, beware or you may be deprived of your brothers and cause my old age to descend with sadness into the grave."

He answered her, "Don't be afraid my blessed mother. I am about to fight with this enemy of God much more than you expect."

Then he approached and stood before Antiochus and said to him, "Why do you pause, accursed butcher? Bring out your sharp sword and cover your hands in my innocent blood."

Antiochus answered, "Eat, my son, from the sacrifice, and I will make you second in my kingdom."

Then the holy one laughed and replied, "Why do you advise me to do that which will not profit me? I will not be turned aside from the path of my brothers and my loved ones. Instead, quickly kill me so I may go to them"

Antiochus ordered, "Put out your hands that they can be chopped off," and he put them out.

He said, "Put out your tongue so it can be cut off," and he put it out.

When his hands and tongue were cut off, he immediately gave up his mind joyously.

We have done great injustice to the struggles of the saints, as we covered their stories so quickly through shortness of time as the holy apostle said, "The time is too short for me to tell of the triumphs of the righteous," so we briefly tell the story of these seven brothers, and we come with few words to this seventh saint. For Satan was not defeated worse by Job than Antiochus was derided by these illustrious ones.

When he saw the seventh one prepared for battle like his brothers, he left him alone and turned to Shamoni and said, "Persuade this child to leave this foolishness and spare your own old age. Keep for yourself this support for your old age, so that you can lean on him. Why do you not have a heart? Why have you no bowels of compassion like other women? Leave yourself one lamp so he can give light to you. Leave yourself one grain of wheat in your field. I myself greatly pity your old age. Behold you have shown in these six who are gone that you love your God. Spare this one who remains to you and follow my orders. Do you have a heart of stone? Don't you feel? Go persuade this one to follow my orders. I swear by all the gods that he will be second in my kingdom. I know that he will do your will and not despise your counsel."

The evil one did not know that Shamoni was unlike her foremother, the weak Eve. When she heard the prophecy of this diviner of Ba'als,[17] she answered him, "I will persuade him."

She turned to her son, mocked the wicked one, and said to him in the language of the forefathers so the evil one did not know what she was saying and heard only the sound of the persuasive words. She said to her son, "I ask of you, my son, to have compassion on me. I carried you for nine months in my womb, and I risked my life giving birth to you, and I carried you in my arms and suckled you for three years, and I raised you until now. Do not repay me a debt for the loans that I lent to you in good faith."

God forbid that your crown should die by your hands! God forbid, lamb, that you should be separated from the flock of your brothers and become food for wolves! God forbid, starlight, that you should be extinguished and fall from the firmament! God forbid, warrior, that you should fall in the battle! God forbid, Sabbath,[18] that you should be seduced from all of your brothers! For on you was proclaimed rest for the Creator who does not tier. Like on the seventh day, the heavens and the earth were finished, and all the army of them. In you, my seventh son ended my labor and struggles, and my womb stopped bearing children. After your birth, the pains of birth no longer distressed me. You are the seal to the crown of your brothers in the kingdom of the sky."

Then the holy one answered his mother, "Get away from me, you nuisance, why do you hold me back from the company of my brothers, the ready merchants? Know that their ships have docked in a safe haven, and I am still drifting among the storms. Was it not enough that I came out of the womb after all of them? See, I must now enter into the kingdom of the sky after all of them. How is it in this I have this great honor, even though I am the youngest in the inheritance, that our good God does not require a full age of faithfulness and good works, but a youth?"

Then he demanded of the persecutors, "Why do you stand still? Kill me quickly that I may go to my brothers because I do not desire the life that dies and grows weak. Now empty your quiver of arrows against me, and all your threats and kill me so I may go and see He whom I love. Furnish me with the afflictions with which crowns are bought in that place. Don't reduce my tortures, or my repayment may be less than that of my brothers."

Then the ravening wolf attacked the blameless lamb in his fury and commanded his servants to torture him however they wanted. They seized him like wild animals. One pulled out his eyes. One cut off his ears. One tore his arms off his sides. One cut out his tongue. When his limbs were cut off, his mind flew with joy to his brothers.

Shamoni is worthy of good remembrance. When she saw her seven sons crowned in one day, she gave thanks and praised God, because she trusted that her offering was accepted before her creator. Yet the evil Antiochus did not respect her old age but tortured her greatly. She rejoiced greatly at this, that not only in her youth she had served God but also in her old age. After she had survived a lot of torture her mind flew to be with her loved ones.

We have told a short story of these holy ones. God did not avert his eyes from them because of their sins, but so their joy and faith might be seen. He delivered others in order that his might would be declared and the greatness of his grace. The three who were saved were not more righteous or better than the seven. Their righteousness was worthy as their confession was worthy of reward, but God averted his eyes from his servants that their truth might be proclaimed.

The holy ones were crowned on the first day of the month of Av[19] through their prayers. May we all be thought worthy to become their companions!

Amen.

The story of Lady Shamoni and her Seven Sons is complete.

7th Maccabees Notes

1 Syriac: mrtîm (ܡܪܬܝܡ)

Her name switched between mrtîm (ܡܪܬܝܡ), used here, and mrîm (ܡܪܝܡ) or mrtå (ܡܪܬܐ) used in other places in the poem. Mrtå (ܡܪܬܐ) was the Syriac word for 'lady' or 'noble woman,' which was adopted as the name Martha (Μάρθα) in Greek, and spread into most European languages. As a result, her name is sometimes translated as 'Martha,' with both mrîm and mrtîm dismissed as scribal errors. Nevertheless, mrtîm (מרתים) was the Judeo-Aramaic word for 'ladies,' suggesting the word is not an error, but a transliteration from an older source text. The Syriac form of Aramaic used simpler pluralization, and mrtå (ܡܪܬܐ) was both the singular and plural form of the word 'lady/ladies.' Her name is rendered in 6th Maccabees as Lady Shamoni (ܡܪܬܐ ܫܡܘܢܝ), which supports this reading.

Therefore, the terms mrtîm (מֹֹתִֹים) or mrtå (מֹתֹא) are both translated as the title 'lady' in this translation. It is unclear why the term would have been pluralized in the original Judeo-Aramaic text unless there were originally more than one lady in the text. It suggests her original name was Mary Shamone (מרים שמונה), however, this name is not consistent with Judean or Aramaic naming conventions from the era. If Mary was a mistranslation of mrtîm (מרתים), then this likely originated as a reference to eight noble women, not one. If so, the original title of this work was *The Story of the Ladies and Their Seven Sons*.

2 Syriac: mrîm (מֹרִֹים). Translation: Mary

Her name switched between mrîm (מֹרִֹים), used here, and mrtîm (מֹֹתִֹים) or mrtå (מֹתֹא) used in other places in the poem. Mrtå (מֹתֹא) was the Syriac word for 'lady' or 'noble woman,' which was adopted as the name Martha (Μάρθα) in Greek, and spread into most European languages. As a result, her name is sometimes translated as 'Martha,' with both mrîm and mrtîm dismissed as scribal errors. Nevertheless, mrtîm (מרתים) was the Judeo-Aramaic word for 'ladies,' suggesting the word is not an error, but a transliteration from an older source text. The Syriac form of Aramaic used simpler pluralization, and mrtå (מֹתֹא) was both the singular and plural form of the word 'lady/ladies.' Her name is rendered in 6th Maccabees as Lady Shamoni (מֹדֹא שׁמֹוֹנִ), which supports this reading.

Therefore, the terms mrtîm (מרתים) or mrtå (מרתא) are both translated as the title 'lady' in this translation. It is unclear why the term would have been pluralized in the original Judeo-Aramaic text unless there were originally more than one lady in the text. The name Mary is rendered in this verse, as that is the name in the Syriac source. It suggests her original name was Mary Shamone (מרים שמונה), however, this name is not consistent with Judean or Aramaic naming conventions from the era. If Mary was a mistranslation of mrtîm (מרתים), then this likely originated as a reference to eight noble women, not one.

3 Syriac: åntîûkůś (ܐܢܛܝܘܟܘܣ). Translation: Antiochus

This is a reference to Antiochus IV Epiphanes, king of the Seleucid Kingdom of Syria between 175 and 164 BC. He died while campaigning in Armenia, in the year 164 BC.

4 Syriac: mšîhå (ܡܫܝܚܐ). Translation: savior (or Messiah, Christ)

5 Syriac: åîåôl (ܐܝܥܠ)

The woman's name was Ya'el (יָעֵל) in the Leningrad Codex, and Îôlå (ܝܥܠ) in the Peshitta. Her name is generally anglicized as Jael from the Greek translation of Iaêl (Ιαήλ).

6 Syriac: ôlîphrnå (ܐܠܝܦܪܢܐ)

The man's name was Olophernês (Ὀλοφέρνης) in the Septuagint. His name is generally anglicized as Holofernes from the Latin translation of his name.

7 Syriac: bbl (ܒܒܠ). Translation: Babylon

The Greek version of the story of Judith claims that Nebuchadnezzar was the king of Assyria, based in Nineveh. There were two Babylonian kings named Nebuchadnezzar the original who ruled between 1121 and 1100 BC, and his namesake Nebuchadnezzar II, who ruled between 605 and 562 BC. Nebuchadnezzar II was the king who ultimately destroyed Jerusalem in 586 BC, after conquering the kingdom of Judah. Over a decade earlier, in 598 BC, Nebuchadnezzar had laid siege to Jerusalem, taken King Jeconiah captive, and placed his uncle Zedekiah on the throne as his regent. Zedekiah declared himself king and formed an alliance with several other Canaanite lands that rebelled against Babylonian authority in 597 BC. There are several versions of the Book of Judith, including a Hebrew translation that appears to have been reworked during the Maccabean Revolt, and a Hebrew translation of the Greek version dating to the Medieval era. This reference to Nebuchadnezzar as the king of Babylon supports the existence of another Aramaic version of the book, likely dating to the Persian era, when the kings of Babylon were being vilified.

There was no known Assyrian king named Nebuchadnezzar. It is believed by most scholars that this is a cryptic reference to the Seleucid Dynasty king Antiochus IV Epiphanes, who declared himself God and tried to ban all other gods. The Nebuchadnezzar found in the other books of the Septuagint was King Nebuchadnezzar II of the Neo-Babylonian Empire between 605 and 562 BC. Nebuchadnezzar II was the son of Nabopolassar, an Assyrian official who rebelled against Assyria in 626 BC. Nebuchadnezzar II was the chief architect of the Neo-Babylonian Empire, who in 605 BC, after taking the throne, launched an invasion of Assyria and Syria with his Median allies, and defeated the Assyrians and Egyptians, and incorporated Syria and Phoenicia into his Empire.

If the original text does date back to the Assyrian or Median Empires, then the original name of the king in the story must have been replaced with a more famous king at some point. A similar set of substitutions took place with the Book of Tobit, which is reflected between the two surviving copies, the common version found in the Codex Vaticanus and most other copies of the Septuagint, and the version in the Codex Sinaiticus, which is substantially different. The Sinaiticus version appears to be an older translation of Tobit, done in a different dialect than used at the Library of Alexandria, which someone decided to include in the Codex Sinaiticus instead of the Alexandrian translation. The Sinaiticus version includes a historically valid version of the conquest of Nineveh by the Medes, while the Vaticanus version claims that the Babylonian King Nebuchadnezzar and the Persian King Xerxes (Ahasuerus / Ασυηρος) destroyed Nineveh, which is nonsense, as they lived a century apart, and neither destroyed Nineveh. Unfortunately, no known variant of Judith exists for comparison.

If this was originally a story written during the Assyrian or Median eras, the Assyrian king in question had to have been Ashurbanipal, who ruled Assyria between 668 and 627 BC. Several parallels are found between Ashurbanipal and the king in Judith, including the war against Elam, the general rebellion throughout his empire, and the conquest of Media, which resulted in the killing of the Median king. The only Assyrian king to do this was Ashurbanipal in year 17 of his reign, the same year listed in the book of Judith, who killed the Median king Phraortes (𒆍𒂍𒌍𒈨𒀭𒌓��), which the book of Judith calls Arphaxad. In the same year, 653 BC, the Egyptians revolted with the aid of the Lydians, who broke their alliance with Assyria, and the following year Babylonia revolted with the backing of the Elamites. It is unclear how much of the Assyrian Empire revolted, however, Ashurbanipal spent years campaigning across his empire to restore it and never bothered trying to recapture Egypt, into which he had sent multiple armies to defend it from Kushite invasions earlier in his reign, before appointing Psamtik I as its pharaoh and slowly withdrawing his troops to suppress the rebellions across the empire.

8 Syriac: mrtå (ܡܪܬܐ). Translation: lady (or female noble)

Her name switched between mrtå (ܡܪܬܐ), used here, and mrtîm (ܡܪܬܝܡ) or mrîm (ܡܪܝܡ), used in other places in the poem. Mrtå (ܡܪܬܐ) was the Syriac word for 'lady' or 'noble woman,' which was adopted as the name Martha (Μάρθα) in Greek and spread into most European languages. As a result, her name is sometimes translated as 'Martha,' with both mrîm and mrtîm dismissed as scribal errors. Nevertheless, mrtîm (מרתים) was the Judeo-Aramaic word for 'ladies,' suggesting the word is not an error but a transliteration from an older source text. The Syriac form of Aramaic used simpler pluralization, and mrtå (ܡܪܬܐ) was both the singular and plural form of the word 'lady/ladies.' Her name is rendered in 6th Maccabees as Lady Shamoni (ܡܪܬܐ ܫܡܘܢܝ), which supports this reading.

9 Syriac: šmônî (ܫܡܘܢܝ)

The woman was called mrtå Šmônî (ܫܡܘܢܝ) in the Syria poem *Lady Shamoni and the Maccabean Martyrs*, also known as 6th Maccabees. The texts both suggest her original name was Mary Shamone (מרים שמונה), however, this name is not consistent with Judean or Aramaic naming conventions from the era. If Mary was a mistranslation of mrtîm (מרתים), then this likely originated as a reference to eight noble women, not one. In this verse, the reference to her name appears to be a scribal note and is, therefore, in parentheses.

10 Syriac: šyôl (ܫܝܘܠ). Translation: Sheol (the underworld)

Sheol was the ancient Canaanite name of the underworld, which was interpreted as Tartarus in the Hellenistic era.

11 Syriac: ḥbîbå (ﻢﺤﺒﺤﺳ). Translation: beloved (or agreeable)

The term is sometimes translated as the name Habib, based on the Arabic name Ḥabīb (حَبِيب). While the Arabic name is derived from the Syriac word, the Syriac word was never interpreted as a name by the other ancient translations that were based on the Judeo-Aramaic texts of Maccabees. The original Judeo-Aramaic term was most likely the same word, ḥbîbå (חביבא), also meaning 'beloved' or 'dear.'

12 Syriac: bsîlåsq (ﻖﺳﻼﻴﺴﺑ). Translation: basilisk

The Greek term basiliscos (βασιλίσκος) was imported into Aramaic as bsîlåsq (𐤐𐤔𐤍𐤋𐤏𐤑𐤏), which was later imported to Latin as basilisk. The original Greek term means 'lesser prince,' and was used as an insult between the rival kings during the Diadochi Wars. The term took on the same meaning as the Greek trôglodytês (τρωγλοδύτης) during the Hellenistic era, which was borrowed back into Greek. The Romans later interpreted the term as a synonym of dracôn (δράκων), resulting in the medieval concept of the basilisk dragon. The earliest reference to the basilisk monster was in Pliny the Elder's Natural History, written in Latin circa 80 AD, however, he described the basilisk as a monstrous cow that killed anyone who saw it. This may have been a historic reference to the Eurasian muskox which, is believed to have gone extinct in Siberia around 550 BC.

As the dating of the text is unclear, there are several possible interpretations. At the time of the event, the term in

Greek would have been a disrespectful title to apply to one of the Hellenistic kings. By the beginning of the Christian era, the term would have been the equivalent of 'troglodyte.' Later in the Byzantine era, the translation would have been the equivalent of 'dragon.' As the text is set during the Hellenistic era, but the term is being used as an insult, the translation of 'troglodyte' is used.

13 Syriac: rqîôå (ܪܩܝܥܐ). Translation: vaulted sky (or celestial sphere)

The rqîôå is the ancient concept of the solid sky that held up the celestial waters. The earliest reference described the sky as being made of lapis lazuli, which, when found on Earth, was believed to be pieces of the sky that had fallen to Earth. By the late Bronze Age, the vaulted sky was recognized as being made from bronze, as it changed colors, appearing like blue unpolished bronze during the day and polished copper bronze in the morning and evening. The Greek philosophers theorized the sky was made of seven crystal spheres, in which the Sun, Moon, and five known planets were located. Above these crystal spheres were the stars in the celestial sea. This model of the universe was adopted by the early Orthodox church and considered the correct interpretation of the universe until the Renaissance. In the Middle East, Jewish scholars developed a ten-level version of the rakia' (רְקִיעַ), which included extra spheres for the stars, comets, and God.

14 Syriac: śûpå (ܣܘܦܐ). Translation: limit (or end, edge)

The word śûpå meant 'edge' or 'limit' in Aramaic, which suggests the original meaning referred to the freshwater subterranean sea below the world in ancient Mesopotamian cosmology. This meaning was incorporated into Mandaeism, a religion based on the teachings of John the Baptist, where the śûpå (ܣܘܦܐ) sea was described as being the sea below the world.

The word was imported to Hebrew as sof (סוֹף), also meaning 'limit' or 'edge,' however, this was also the name of the suf (סוּף) sea from the Torah, which was based on the Egyptian word tjûfî (𓏏�𓈖), meaning 'papyrus' or 'reeds.' This has led to the Syriac and Mandiac words śûpå also being translated as 'papyrus' or 'reeds.' This translation uses the original meaning of the Syriac word.

15 Syriac: śtnyn (ܣܛܢܝܢ). Translation: satans (or devils, rivals, adversaries)

The term stnå (ܣܛܢܐ) was used in medieval Syriac, the same as the word šaytān (شَيْطَان) Arabic, as a reference to demons and genies that oppose God. In the older Aramaic usage, stnå (ܢܛܕܝ) had the same meaning as the Hebrew satan (שָׂטָן), meaning 'contender' or 'adversary.' As the origin of the text is not clear, the term is simply transliterated as 'satans.'

16 Syriac: årûbtå (ܥܪܘܒܬܐ). Translation: Friday (or Aphrodite, Allat)

17 Syriac: bůlîm (ܒܥܠܝܡ). Translation: lords (or husbands, ba'als)

The ba'als, meaning lords, were the old gods of the Canaanite civilization.

18 Syriac: šbtå (ܫܒܬܐ). Translation: sabbath

19 Syriac: åb (ܐܒ). Translation: Av

Av (אָב) is the fifth month of the ecclesiastical year in the Jewish calendar. The month was adopted by the Judeans and Arameans from the Neo-Babylonians, who called it the month of Abu (𒌚𒉈). The month of Av corresponds with late July and early August on the Gregorian calendar.

8th Maccabees

During the rule of Antiochus Epiphanes,[1] when many of the people of the city had died from a plague, a priest called Leius ordered a rock on the mountain above the city to be carved into an enormous masked head facing the city and the valley. He wrote an inscription on it, following which the deaths from the plague stopped. Up until the present time, the people of Antioch call this head Charonion.[2]

Antiochus Epiphanes was the first to build the so-called government house outside the city limits of Great Antioch. Here all the councilors met with all the statesmen and all the property-holders of the city, to debate what to do about whatever occurred, and then to provide anything that was required. Antiochus constructed some other buildings outside the city and called this area Epiphania after his own name. He did not put a wall around it, but it was built on the mountain.

Antiochus Epiphanes was angry with Ptolemy,[3] the king of Egypt, because Ptolemy demanded taxes from the Judeans, who lived in his territory. The Judeans came to Antioch from Palestine[4] and asked Antiochus to write to Ptolemy, the ruler and king of Egypt, that he should not demand tariffs from the Judeans as they were importing grain for their survival. There was a great famine in Palestine at the time, and therefore the

Judeans were importing grain from the land of Egypt. When Ptolemy received Antiochus' letter, he ordered that the Judeans should pay more tariffs.

Then Antiochus Epiphanes marched against Ptolemy because he had ignored his letter. There was a battle between them, in which many of Antiochus' soldiers were killed, and he fled back to the borders of his own territory. When the Judeans in Jerusalem heard of this, they agreed to terms with Ptolemy and surrendered to him, because they thought that Antiochus had died. But Antiochus Epiphanes had gathered another army and attacked Ptolemy. He destroyed his army and killed him. When Antiochus heard what the Judeans in Jerusalem had done, as if they had celebrated his defeat, he marched against Jerusalem.

He besieged the city and captured it, then slaughtered all the inhabitants. He took high priest Eleazar[5] of Judea, along with the Maccabees[6] back to Antioch, where he sentenced them to death. He abolished the high priesthood of Judea, and he rededicated the Judeans' temple, which had been built by Solomon, into a temple of the Olympian Zeus[7] and Athena.[8] He defiled the building with meat and prevented the Judeans from performing their ancestral acts of worship. For three years, he forced them to follow Greek customs.

When Antiochus died, his son Antiochus Glaucus,[9] who was called the hawk,[10] became king for two years.

After him, Demetrius[11] the son of Seleucus was king for eight years. A Judean called Judas[12] came to Great Antioch and shamed Demetrius with his claims so much that the king handed over the temple and the remains of the Maccabees to him. Judas buried the Maccabees in the so-called Ceratium in Great Antioch, where there was a synagogue of the Judeans. Antiochus had punished the Maccabees a short way outside the city of Antioch, on the 'ever-weeping' mountain opposite the temple of Zeus Casius.[13] Then Judas purified the temple and refounded Jerusalem, celebrating a Passover feast in honor of God. This was the second capture of Jerusalem, as Eusebius the follower of Pamphilus recorded in his chronicle.

8th Maccabees Notes

1 Greek: Antiochos Epiphanês (Αντϕοχoc Επιϕλνρc)

Antiochus IV Epiphanes was the king of the Selucid Empire between 175 to 164 BC.

2 Greek: Charônion (χαϸοoνιoν)

The masked head still exists on the mountainside above Antakya, Turkey. The head is quite weathered after 2300 years and appears to have been vandalized at some point, so it is not clear what the mask originally looked like. The name is based on the name of the ancient Canaanite psychopomp Hrn (𐤇𐤓𐤍 / 𐤉𐤀𐤇), who was later known as Ḥûǎrûn (𐡇𐡅𐡓𐡍) in Egyptian, and Charôn (Χαρων) in Greek. The suffix of -ιον suggests the city was being rededicated to Charon, however, the name was not changed. If there were words carved into the rock, they are no longer visible.

3 Greek: Ptolemaeos (ⲡⲧⲟⲗⲉⲙⲁⲓⲟⲥ)

Ptolemy VI Philometor was the king of Egypt between 180 and 164 BC, and again between 163 and 145 BC.

4 Greek: Palaestinê (ⲡⲁⲗⲁⲓⲥⲧⲓⲛⲏ)

Judea was renamed Palestine by the Romans after they conquered Judea during the Second Judean-Roman War.

5 Greek: Eleazar (ⲉⲗⲉⲁⲍⲁⲣ)

In 2nd Maccabees and other older Greek sources, this high priest was called Jason (Ἰάσων). In the late 1st century AD, Josephus claimed this priest had changed his name from Jesus (Ἰησοῦς / ישוע‎), the Aramaic form of Joshua (יְהוֹשֻׁעַ‎). Eleazar was a different person in 2nd Maccabees, who died at the same time. At some point between the 2nd century BC, and the 4th century AD, the two were conflated in the Syriac tradition, which John was using as a source.

6 Greek: Maccabaeoe (ܡܲܟ̇ܟ̇ܵܕ̇ܝܼܵܝܹܐ)

Maccabee (Μακκαβαῖος) is the nickname of Judas, the son of Mattathias, in the Septuagint's 1st Maccabees, as well as Hebrew and Arabic Maccabees. However, his rebellion started as a response to the events described, and this version of the story refers to more than one Maccabees (Μακκαβαιοι). The association of Eleazar with the Maccabees indicates that this reference was to the seven martyrs, who are called the Maccabees in the Syriac poem Martha Shamoni and the Maccabean Martyrs, also known academically as 6th Maccabees. The story of the murder of the seven martyrs is also found in the Septuagint's 2nd Maccabees, as well as the Hebrew and Arabic books of Maccabees, however, they are not called the Maccabees in those books, indicating that the identification was specific to the Syriac tradition.

7 Greek: Zeus Olympios (ܙܘܿܣ ܐܘܿܠܘܿܡܦܝܘܿܣ)

Zeus Olympios was a title of Zeus that denoted he was the Zeus worshipped at Mount Olympus. The name Zeus derives from deus (δεύς), the Greek word for 'god,' and was applied to several other gods during the Hellenic era. The god in question is called Dios Olympiou (Διος Ολυμπιου) in the Septuagint's 2nd Maccabees.

8 Greek: Athêna (ܐܬܢܐ)

Athena was the daughter of Zeus and the Greek version of the ancient Canaanite virgin goddess Ônt (𐤏𐤍𐤕 / 𐡏𐡍𐡕), the

Egyptian Ôntît (𓏏𓈖𓏏𓆇), and the Israelite goddess of wisdom Ônt (𓏏𓈖𓏏), all of which are generally anglicized as Anat. Anat was worshiped by the Israelites in Egypt until at least the 5th century BC, as evidenced by the Elephantine papyri, but is not mentioned as late as the Maccabean Revolt. None of the other books of the Maccabees support Athena being worshiped in Jerusalem, however, as she was Zeus' daughter, it is plausible her cult was present.

9 Greek: Antiochos Glaucos (Ⲁⲛⲧⲫⲟⲭⲟⲥ Ⲅⲗⲁⲩⲕⲟⲥ)

The heir to Antiochus IV Epiphanes was Antiochus V Eupator (Αντίοχος Ευπάτωρ), who ruled between 172 and 161 BC. Eupator is a later epithet applied to the king that translates as 'our good father.'

The Septuagint manuscripts record two versions of the: Ypaton Antiochon (Υπατον Αντιοχον) and Eypatora Antiochon (Ευπατορα Αντιοχον), indicating the name Glaucos (Γλαυκος) was imported from an Aramaic source. Glaucos was a Greek sea god of prophecy whose name was used by many Greeks.

10 Greek: hierax (ⲓⲧⲣⲁⲍ).

• Translation: hawk

Hierax is the Greek word meaning hawk, which was used by cunning leaders. It was used as a name or nickname by the Seleucid dynasty, including Antiochus Hierax, a prince who seized control of the Selucid's territories in Anatolia between 245 and 226 BC.

11 Greek: Dêmêtrios (ΔΗΜΗΤΡΙΟϹ)

Demetrius I Soter (Δημήτριος Σωτήρ) was the king of the Selucid Empire between 162 and 150 BC.

12 Greek: Ioudas (ΙΟΥΔΑϹ).

- Translation: Judas (or Judah)

Judah the son of Mattathias, was the leader of the Maccabean revolt between 167 and 160 BC.

13 Greek: Casion (ΚΑϹΙΟΝ)

Mount Casion is the ancient Greek name of the mountain near Antioch. It was known as Ḫaazzi ([illegible]) in Akkadian, Ḫazi ([illegible]) in Hurrian, Djåpônå ([illegible]) in Egyptian, Zabuna ([illegible]) in Middle Babylonian, Ṣpn ([illegible] / 𐤑𐤐𐤍) in Phoenician, and Ṣpůn (צפון) in Aramaic. The temple of Ba'al Hadad, the ancient Canaanite storm god, was located on the mountain, indicating that the Zeus of Casion was originally Ba'al Hadad.

Also Available

ALSO AVAILABLE

ENOCH AND METATRON SERIES:
- Books of Enoch Collection
- Books of Enoch and Metatron Collection
- Books of Metatron Collection
- Secrets of Enoch

OTHER TRANSLATIONS:
- Apocalypses of Ezra
- Arabic Maccabees
- Hebrew Maccabees
- Life of Adam and Eve
- Memories of the New Kingdom
- Septuagint's Esther and the Vetus Latina Esther
- Septuagint's Ezekiel and the Ba'al Cycle
- Septuagint's Job and the Testament of Job
- Septuagint's Proverbs and the Wisdom of Amenemope
- Syriac Maccabees - Deuterocanonical Books
- The Amarna Letters
- Testaments of the Patriarchs Collection
- Tobit and Ahikar
- Ugaritic Texts: Ba'al Cycle
- Wisdom of Ahikar